DATE DUE

DEC 17 '73	

George N. Patterson

A Scottish engineer foreman and medical missionary, George Patterson was in Tibet during Communist operation. Remaining in Asia as a journalist after mainland China fell to Communism, he has written nine books, numerous articles, and has served as TV consultant to BBC on Asian affairs.

CHRISTIANITY
in
COMMUNIST CHINA

CHRISTIANITY
in
COMMUNIST CHINA

GEORGE N. PATTERSON

WORD BOOKS, Publisher

Waco, Texas   London, England

First Printing—March 1969
Second Printing—September 1970

CHRISTIANITY IN COMMUNIST CHINA

Library of Congress Catalog Card Number 69-12818
Printed in the United States of America

O Lord, thou hast deceived me, and I was deceived: thou art stronger than I, and hast prevailed: I am in derision daily, every one mocketh me.

For since I spake, I cried out, I cried violence and spoil; because the word of the Lord was made a reproach unto me, and a derision, daily.

Then I said, I will not make mention of him, nor speak any more in his name. But his word was in mine heart as a burning fire shut up in my bones, and I was weary with forbearing, and I could not stay.

For I heard the defaming of many, fear on every side. Report, say they, and we will report it. All my familiars watched for my halting, saying, Peradventure he will be enticed, and we shall prevail against him, and we shall take our revenge on him.

But the Lord is with me as a mighty, terrible one: therefore my persecutors shall stumble, and they shall not prevail: they shall be greatly ashamed; for they shall not prosper: their everlasting confusion shall never be forgotten.

But, O Lord of hosts, that triest the righteous, and seest the reins and the heart, let me see thy vengeance on them: for unto thee have I opened my cause.

Sing unto the Lord, praise ye the Lord: for he hath delivered the soul of the poor from the hand of evildoers.

—Jeremiah 20:7-13

CONTENTS

PREFACE

TO BE IN CHINA in 1949 was to be a spectator of the death throes of a nation and the end of a tortured epoch; or of the shrugging off of a useless chrysalis and the beginning of a promising new era. It depended on whether one was north or south of the Yangtze River, East or West in one's ideological loyalties, left or right in one's political bias. For to the north of the Yangtze River a new force in Chinese affairs was gathering, a new ideology was taking shape, a new China was emerging—the creation of persons and policies of China's first Communist government.

In the summer of 1949 Mao Tse-tung made his now famous speech declaring firmly that New China "leaned to one side"—that it aligned itself with the Soviet Union. In Peking the new Communist leaders convened a conference of all parties to discuss a common program on the basis of which the new government of China was to be proclaimed. On October 1, 1949, the Central Government of the People's Republic of China was proclaimed from the Square of the Tien An-men, the "Gate of Heavenly Peace," with Mao Tse-tung as Chairman and Chou En-lai as Prime Minister and Foreign Minister.

The new era was about to begin. A new creed, a new spirit, a new orthodoxy, new alignments, new methods, a new vision of Chinese world empire were the themes of all political discussions. They caught the imagination of the long-tormented, humiliated, and frustrated Chinese people with their magic and promise.

The Communist Party had established itself as the largest single force in mobilizing, developing, and directing a large section of the Chinese people as instruments of change for better conditions. They had proved indisputably that they were fitted to do the same with the rising energies of the new age. Nor were they merely successful exponents of a comparatively new Western ideology in a corrupt and effete Eastern environment, tied slavishly to the dogma, dicta, and example of the first Communist nation, Russia. They had hammered out their own creed through years of practical experiment, in the face of often bitter opposition from Stalin and despite fundamental differences of opinion with the theories of Lenin.

It was with this attitude of mind that the Communist Party of China, riding on the crest of the revolutionary tide in 1949, called a national convention in September known as the Chinese People's Political Committee. They planned to translate their vision of a Chinese socialist utopia into reality and to forge the Chinese people into a weapon for Chinese world empire.

Against this background the statement of a noted Chinese historian, C. K. Yang, that "the only organized religion by which the Communists [in China] feel threatened is Christianity" seemed a pretentious and puny defiance.[1]

Fifteen months after taking over power in China, the new government regime seemed to have disposed effectively and finally with this supposed threat. One international news magazine summed it up:

The Bamboo Curtain fell harshly last week on a century of good works in China. Red China's Vice-Chairman of the State Administrative Council, Kuo Mo-jo, charged:
"American imperialism has, over a long period, placed special emphasis on . . . cultural aggression in China."
Kuo recommended and the Peking regime approved:
1. A ban on U.S. subsidies for China's schools and churches.
2. A take-over by the Red State, or by "puppet people's" enterprises, of all U.S.-subsidized educational, medical and relief institutions.
3. A transfer of U.S.-subsidized "religious bodies" to the control of the Chinese believers [whom] the government should encourage to become independent, self-sufficient and self-preaching (sic).
Kuo reckoned that the properties had been worth $41,900,000.
Among the chief "cultural aggressors," the twelve Protestant "Christian Colleges" run by the United Board for Christian Colleges in China; the Peking Union Medical College and Chang-sha's "Yale in China" which were beacon lights of modern medicine in China; and the Catholic schools and mission churches that have served 3,500,000 Chinese Catholics. U.S. religious bodies had supported and operated 506 hos-

x

CHAPTER ONE

The Subversion of Christianity:
An Inside Account

I ARRIVED IN HONG KONG in July 1964 during the filming of a television series. I was the adviser and script writer of the unit. We had just been filming the Tibetan guerillas in action against the Chinese Communists inside Tibet, and were in the process of doing a different type of film about the growth and distribution channels of the opium trade. After completing a few more films, we intended to return to Britain.

However, while in Hong Kong I felt very strongly that God wanted me to remain there. Professionally this was a most difficult decision to make, for my political experience was in West Asia, and just to remain in Hong Kong—where there was an abundance of internationally known Far East correspondents—meant a blind step into an unknown future. I wrote to my wife who had our three young children (four years, two years, and six months) to find out how she felt, and she agreed to come to Hong Kong.

During this period I met a Chinese journalist, Jack Chow, former news editor of a Hong Kong English language daily and radio correspondent for Voice of America, who was a deeply committed Christian. As our friendship increased, both professionally and spiritually, he was concerned that my time and writing talent should not be wasted in Hong Kong. Although I was already working on a book, I had no journalistic appointment.

One day he brought me news of a contact he had made with a refugee who had recently fled from China. Because of his importance he was being kept under strict surveillance in Hong Kong, was using several aliases for protection, and was hoping to get to the United States. He had been passed to Jack for debriefing by interpretation. Jack was aware that the information at his disposal would make an excellent book about conditions of religious practice inside Communist China. Through Jack, I was able to meet secretly with this official and to discuss his background and developments in the religious situation in China since 1949.

Hsiao Feng—to use one of his names—was an important Chinese Communist Party official who for several years had held a senior post in charge of religious policy before escaping to Hong Kong. He was the son of a Chinese Nationalist Army colonel by his "third" wife. His father, a graduate of the Whampoa Military Academy in Canton, had been a regimental commander fighting the Japanese in 1943 and a divisional adjutant fighting the Chinese Communists in 1949. After the fall of Canton he escaped to Hong Kong.

Hsiao Feng had an erratic education, due partly to his father's movements and partly to the unsettled conditions, but he graduated from Yu Fen Middle School in Loting, Western Kwangtung, in 1945. Hsiao had a deep interest in literature, and he joined a book reading club which specialized in left-wing literature. As he avidly read the works of Pa Chin, Mao Tun, Gorki, Turgenev and Chekhov, Balzac, Goethe, Dreiser, and Howard Fast, he was led gradually but inevitably into communism.

In 1949, with the help of a relative, he was put in touch with a Chinese Communist sympathizer in Hong Kong who advised him to return to Canton "to strengthen yourself ideologically" while waiting out "the period of darkness before dawn." One week after the Communist entry into Canton on October 14, 1949, he was introduced by his relative to the chief of personnel of the newly established Municipal People's Government and enrolled for membership in the "Youth League and the School for Administrative Cadres." In the spring of 1950 he was assigned to the Civil Affairs Bureau of the Municipal People's Government, with the duties of registrar of civic organs, religious bodies, relief and welfare organizations, guilds and clubs in the city.

In November 1951 after a spell of duty in the Municipal Public Security Bureau, Hsiao Feng was transferred to the Propaganda Department of the Canton Party Committee. There his assignment was to help prepare for the establishment of a separate Religious Affairs Department under the Municipal Government. After two months of intensive preparations the Religious Affairs Department of the Canton Municipal Government was established, with Hsiao Feng as a section chief.

In accordance with directives from the Central Government, this "organ," while carrying the label of a "government unit," was in fact placed under the direct control of the United Front Work Department as the Propaganda Department of the local Party committee. Cadres to staff the new organ were carefully selected by rigorous examinations. Almost all were drawn from the Party Committee's United Front Work Department, the Propaganda Department, and the city government's Public Security Bureau. Each was a member of either the Party or the Youth League, and had to be "absolutely trustworthy in politics," have "a certain standard of education," and "have experience in investigation and research work." No knowledge of religion was necessary.

Hsiao Feng cited his two colleagues, Ma Hao and Yao Yen, as good examples of the types of person recruited. The former had been chief of a provincial radio station and admitted that he knew nothing of religion. Yao Yen was transferred from a district Party committee where he was director of the Propaganda Department; he also knew nothing of religion. Hsiao himself, in the course of his wide reading, had read religious history; so he was given the job of training the general cadres.

The "organization law" of the Religious Affairs Bureau was given as follows:

(1) To investigate regularly all religious bodies and the activities of their personnel;
(2) To control all types of religious activity;

(3) To lead both Catholics and Protestants into the Three-Self Movement, and to organize Buddhists, Taoists and Muslims for regular study sessions;

(4) To carry out thoroughly the religious policy of the Central Government;

(5) Unceasingly to teach and propagandize religious leaders and all believers concerning the policies of the State with respect to the current situation, in order to raise their political consciousness;

(6) To bring church leaders closer to the government and push believers of all religions into a positive alliance for socialist construction;

(7) To strike at politically obstructive reactionaries in the churches, and co-operate with the public security departments in the suppression of hidden counterrevolutionaries in religious circles;

(8) To entertain foreign religious visitors from abroad.

With the exception of a set of regulations governing the preservation of religious edifices and relics of historical and cultural value, Hsiao Feng said "there was no recognized official measure for implementing the foregoing policy." Civil Affairs officials had only one guide to go by in their work: "The Foundations of Leninism," consisting of a series of lectures by Stalin.

To Hsiao's knowledge the first article that could be considered a "policy statement" on religion by the Chinese Communist Party was published in *Study,* a theoretical journal of the Central Committee's Propaganda Department, in 1950. It was entitled "What Is the Correct Way for Marxist-Leninists to Deal with Religious Problems?" In the article, Lenin's theory that religion is the opiate of the people was discussed, as well as the proposition that the Chinese Communists could cooperate with all religious believers in the task of building a new democracy in China; but little or no practical information was provided.

Hsiao Feng and his colleagues interpreted their function largely for themselves. They ordered every religious organization or unit, such as a church or monastery, to compile a report about its history, table of organization, membership, assets, and property. A record had to be kept of daily congregations. Proceedings of any and all administrative meetings, board meetings, and annual meetings had to be submitted in detail for the inspection of the Religious Affairs Bureau, which sometimes sent cadres to attend such meetings. Every priest or pastor had to submit his sermon to the bureau which censored what it deemed to run contrary to the Party's interests.

When Hsiao Feng spoke to religious leaders or groups of church workers, he confined the propaganda content of his speeches to the Party's policy of "freedom of religious belief." This had the following main points: (1) People who believe in a religion have freedom; (2) people who do not believe in a religion also have freedom, including the freedom to oppose religion (but religious believers usually did not get to hear this clause); (3) people have freedom to change their religious belief.

In practice (2) meant that a religious group could conduct its activity only in its own place of worship; namely, Christians in their church, Buddhists in their monastery or nunnery, Taoists in their temple, etc. The reason given for this restriction was that "it would protect the activities of the religious from being disturbed by the nonreligious, and at the same time protect the nonreligious from being disturbed by the religious." This idea seemed reasonable enough; but it meant that Christians could no longer sing Christmas carols outside their own churches, or distribute religious tracts in public places, or hold meetings on street corners; Buddhists could no longer liberate living creatures out-of-doors for merit; Buddhist or Taoist priests could no longer conduct rituals for the dead in a private home.

This interpretation, which was aimed primarily at curtailing the social influence of the religious worker, affected religious organizations throughout the country in many other ways. For instance, Catholics and Protestants would change their faith as they chose, or an adherent would simultaneously join several churches. Or a believer would introduce some contrary opinions into his own church, openly disputing its accepted doctrines, rules, and practices. Most of the Protestant pastors adopted the dress "of the common people" so that when they were seen in public places their "attire would not create a conflict between the religious and the nonreligious." The Roman Catholics were more conservative and resisted such changes as best they could, but it became increasingly difficult for the priests to enforce discipline. For example, it was no longer possible to compel observance of the church rule that a Catholic could not marry a non-Catholic, or to withhold Holy Communion from one who had violated one of the Ten Commandments.

These conditions reopened old conflicts and fostered new ones between different church groups, and even within each group and sect. There were also conflicts between clergymen, and between clergymen and laymen. According to Hsiao it was the policy of the Communist Party to consider these interdenominational quarrels as "the affairs of the opposing groups." Cadres like himself were constantly reminded never to take sides or to get involved, but to seize the opportunity to maneuver both contending parties into a position where they had to admit themselves in the wrong, and so submit themselves further to the control of the Party.

Since the Party itself was aware that it lacked the experience to deal with the religious problem, it was forever urging caution in its directives to the local committees charged with the direction and supervision of religious work. The standing order at that time was: "The Party neither prohibits nor supports the development of religion, but seeks to actively lead the religious people in carrying out the 'Three-Self Reform Movement' and so gradually reduce the influence of religion."

From the political point of view, therefore, the Religious Affairs Bureau became a "religious self-government office," claimed Hsiao. From the point of view of religious groups it became the leading organization for all religious work. All religions had to obey this organization, which in turn was responsible to the national Religious Affairs Bureau of the State Council, the highest religious organization —the "Kingdom of Religion." This, said Hsiao, was very much like the pagoda-like structure of the Roman Catholic Church: A Roman Catholic church belongs to the diocese, which is under the archdiocese, which is under the Pope, in the Vatican at Rome. The difference is that the Pope is head only of Catholics all over the world, whereas the Religious Affairs Bureau of the State Council of Communist China governs every kind of religion in the whole mainland of China. It is the Chinese Vatican of all religions.

With increasing experience Hsiao Feng came to the conclusion that he doubted Lenin's theory—"government separate from religions, religions separate from government [politics]." Certainly what was taking place in China was "government-managed religious affairs" rather than the "government separate from religion" of Lenin, and what was emerging was simply a propaganda organization for communism.

Hsiao Feng's unsolicited remarks on the origin of the Three-Self Reform Movement (to be dealt with in detail later) were illuminating. He said that the movement was "initiated in 1950 by a group of leftist Christian leaders doing the bidding of the Party, and it remains to this day the most important united front machinery through which the Chinese Communists exercise their control over all religions in China, especially the two main branches of Christianity—the Roman Catholics and Protestants."

The leading initiator of the Three-Self Movement was Wu Yao-tsung of the Y.M.C.A. Wu and the Secretary-General of the China Buddhist Association, Chao Pu-ch'u, were both actually secret numbers of the Communist Party assigned to special tasks. Chao Pu-ch'u, on his return from a visit to Japan, represented the Central Committee of the Communist Party in a secret investigation in Hsiao Feng's area to check what the Municipal Party Committee was doing in certain Buddhist problems. Hsiao Feng was ordered to report to him. Before initiating the Three-Self Movement Wu Yao-tsung received a directive from the director of the Propaganda Department of the Central Committee of the Communist Party, Lu Ting-yi. He was instructed to approach the Christian leaders of Peking, Tientsin, Shanghai, and Kwangchow for signatures to the statement that launched the Three-Self Movement (see Chapter Three).

In Shanghai, where the Roman Catholics were strongly concentrated, Bishop Kung Ping-mei and his priests openly refused to agree to participate in the Three-Self Movement. Bishop Ch'en Yi-hsiu, of the South China Catholic Diocese in Kwangchow (and later Bishop Teng Yi-ming, also) not long after being forced to sign as supporters of the parallel Catholic Three-Self Movement, declared that they were withdrawing because no true Catholic could subscribe to the conditions and it was impossible to combine with Protestants. The South China Diocese, which included Kwangtung, Kwangsi, Hupeh, and Kiangsi provinces, was extremely influential. The director of the Religious Affairs Bureau in Shanghai, Yao Piao-t'ing, was criticized by the Central Committee of the Party in Peking because he "could not break them in after such a long period." The Peking director of the United Front Work Department of the Kwangchow Communist Party Committee, Lo Hua, was also criticized when he failed, even after many meetings and much abuse, to persuade Bishop Ch'en Yi-hsiu to join the Three-Self Movement.

Other examples of the failure to extend the Three-Self Movement in Roman Catholic circles, were Ch'en Chih-hsing, former headmaster of the Catholic Shen Hsiu Middle School in Kwangchow, and Fong Shuo-mei, an engineer. Both were regional members of the Legion of Mary, which was classified by the Communists as a reactionary organization. The Public Security Bureau had planned to arrest them as "leaders of a reactionary organization," but it was decided to use them to arouse revolts in Catholic churches. Instead of being arrested, each had to confess his crimes in writing. Ch'en Chih-hsiing was then appointed master and department head of a government Middle School, and Fong Shuo-mei was assigned to work at the Yangtze River Water Conservation Engineering School and the Municipal Planning Department. The only condition attached to their employment was that they must establish a Three-Self Movement Committee in the Catholic Church.

The two, acting as lay leaders, started a Kwangchow Roman Catholic Three-Self Movement Committee with themselves as directors, but they received no support from the clergy or other church workers. The few members they had in their organization had no influence in the church. By carrying out orders, however, they avoided arrest.

Hsiao Feng claimed that the Korean War made possible the formation of the Three-Self Movement. The Party leaders had been unsuccessful in finding ways, short of repressive methods, to win over the vast majority of religious leaders as well as rank-and-file believers. With the outbreak of the Korean War in June, 1950, they were afraid that the congregations might become a "tool of imperialist aggression." They might form a fifth column working for the enemy within the country if or when China entered the war on the side of the North Koreans. Therefore, as part of the nationwide "Campaign to Resist American Aggression, Aid Korea" the Communist Party put pressure on religious leaders to renounce publicly their foreign associations and adopt anti-Western attitudes. Those who refused were quickly branded as "counterrevolutionaries" or "agents of foreign imperialism" and severely dealt with.

At first church workers were pressured to hold meetings of accusation against "imperialists who have carried out aggression against China under the cloak of religion." Under the direction of cadres, each church or sect would conduct its own accusation meetings in which members would study pertinent documents, analyze them, and then make criticisms. Afterwards all religious workers, regardless of denomination, would be brought together to repeat the same process. When the "aggressive crimes" of the foreign missions had been thoroughly exposed, the religious workers would be asked to get up one by one and solemnly declare that their relationships with their home churches would be severed.

In some cities the accusation meetings went on for two or three months. Each of the participants had to make seven or eight accusations before he was recognized as having "made a clean breast of himself." Most were only able to say that their church was established by some foreign mission, but even this was accepted as evidence that foreign imperialists had used religion for committing aggression against China.

When the "accusation" movement was completed, most of the accusations made by religious workers were reported to the Central Government. These reports were regarded as highly valuable material, for they contained information about the internal affairs of the churches which the authorities very much needed. This material was classified, and the more important materials compiled in a set of pamphlets entitled, "Reference Materials on the Crimes of Imperialists in Using Religion to Commit Aggression Against China." This file was for government use only and was kept confidential. It was used in three ways: (1) to provide clues for the investigation of foreign spy cases by public security organizations in the large cities and outlying provinces; (2) as reference material for the Religious Affairs Bureau in every city, to be used as a tool for control; (3) as a "handbook" for the directors of culture departments of the government and of Party propaganda departments above the district level, so that such people could understand the serious nature of the religious problems of New China. Officials were warned of the words of Lenin that "the customs of millions and millions of people is a most terrible power" and "the religious problem is a most serious and complicated problem." The whole set of "Reference Materials" amounted to ten volumes; but these were later divided into Roman Catholic, Protestant, Buddhist, and other sections.

In July, 1952, Hsiao Feng was seconded to the Propaganda Department of the South China Sub-bureau of the Party Central Committee to assist in mapping out a "campaign for the ideological re-moulding of teachers in institutions of higher learning in Kwang-tung Province." Later he was sent to Sun Yat-sen University, Ling-nan University, and Sun Yat-sen University Medical School to con-duct similar campaigns.

In January, 1953, Hsiao Feng was returned to the Religious Af-fairs Bureau to resume his duties. That same year the first "Na-tional Conference on Religious Work" was held in Peking. It was a secret meeting convened by the Party to review past work and set new tasks for the future. At that meeting one speaker was Hsi Chung-hsun, then a vice-director of the Propaganda Department of the Party's Central Committee. He laid down the guidelines of approach to the problem: "Outright prohibition is useless; it will only hurt our Party. . . . Religion is a form of social consciousness. If we prohibit it by administrative order, fanaticism will result, pos-sibly bringing with it religious riots. Therefore, if we are to destroy it we must do it gradually by other methods."

Hsiao Feng did not attend the conference, for attendance was limited to members of the ruling clique. But he knew what went on at the conference through verbal reports of visiting colleagues or through printed minutes distributed to provincial leaders later.

Hsiao Feng reckoned that it was at the first Conference held in 1953 that decisions were made to "reconstitute" the Three-Self Movement (see Chapter Six). In the autumn of 1953, after many people had expressed great dissatisfaction with the Three-Self Re-form Movement, the Religious Affairs Bureau of the State Council in Peking ordered the name changed from "Three-Self Reform Movement Committee" to "Three-Self Patriotic Movement Com-mittee." The Roman Catholic Church, and such sects as the Chris-tian Assemblies (Little Flock), Ling Liang (Spiritual Food), Evangelistic Mission, and Evangelistic Boat Mission, who had op-posed the Three-Self Reform Movement, as well as Christian pas-tors and workers who were forced to participate in it, did not like the idea of "reform." They understood "reform" to mean that Chris-tians had to accept reform of their *faith* and *church* by Marxist-Leninist doctrine.

In the summer of 1954, Hsiao Feng toured Kwangtung Province to investigate "religious conditions" in Swatow, Chaochow, and various other places. The director of the Propaganda Department of the local Communist Party committee and the detective section of the local Public Security Bureau had given him disturbing reports regarding growing religious activities in these areas. All Catholic and Protestant churches in the towns and villages had been closed, but it appeared that there were "underground home congregations" multiplying in many areas. Hsiao Feng and officials of the Religious Affairs Bureau, together with officials of other departments, began to keep a close watch on these developments.

About this time Hsiao Feng also began to have his own intraparty problems. First he went ahead with some projects without prior approval of the Party superiors; then he was passed over for a high promotion which he was certain was his; then the Party alleged that he had not properly "prepared" Bishop Mu Jung-hsien in Canton for a visit by the British Labour Party Premier, Clement Attlee. Finally, in 1955, Hsiao had written a favorable review of a book—*Battle of the Marshland* by Lu Ling—which had not been favorably reviewed by other leading critics. Hsiao Feng was accused of being "discontented with the Party," of "speaking in a strange tongue," and of "sentimentalism towards religious people."

On August 16, 1955, Hsiao Feng was suspended from his post but given his pay. Every night he was the object of Party "struggle" meetings to make him see the errors of his ways, which he stubbornly refuted. On December 30, 1955, he was sent to the labor camp at Shako, a suburb of Canton, for a term, pending further investigation. After repeated appeals to the authorities for a reinvestigation of his case, he was released on July 20, 1956. On that day two cadres from the Religious Affairs Bureau came to take him straight back to the department, where his return was accepted without comment. Party leaders simply called a meeting to announce apologetically that, as he had been cleared of all charges, he had been reinstated that day. But things could never be quite the same for him again, and for the first time he began to think of possible alternatives.

In the meantime a new directive had been issued after the Second National Conference on Religious Work was held in Peking in 1954. It called for "infusing Marxist-Leninist thought into the positive doctrines of religion." In announcing this directive Ho Cheng-hsiang, director of the Religious Affairs Bureau of the State Council, had declared: "The positive values of patriotism should take the place of negative religious propaganda. We Communists can accept as reasonable certain parts of the Bible which Christians use, but we must also pay attention to the doctrines that they preach. If we infuse those doctrines with our Marxist-Leninist thought, then they will have positive significance and can serve our cause."

The "parts of the Bible" which Communists found reasonable, according to Ho Cheng-hsiang, were the Ten Commandments. He acknowledged that the real purpose of the Bible "was to advocate peace and philanthropy" but added that it had no class standpoint. Finally, he said, "we must oppose sermons on supernatural things, especially subjects like 'the Last Judgment' in Catholicism and 'Jesus will come again' and 'Doomsday' in Protestantism. We must promote propaganda of world peace, patriotism, love of the people, and support for the realistic world."

Pressure was put on every pastor and priest throughout the country to conform to these directives. Articles publicizing the Party's "new stand on religion" were circulated among both clergymen and laymen. Catholic priests and Protestant pastors were told to submit drafts of their sermons for censorship beforehand.

Few dared to defy the authorities, because of yet another measure. The Religious Affairs Bureau had begun to compile a "secret dossier" on every clergyman or administrative worker of a religious organization. In the dossier were kept his photograph, sample of handwriting, biography, and up-to-date account of all his political activities—as well as anything that could be interpreted as "anti-Communist expressions" in his sermons or remarks. The Communist officials took the same care to compile a dossier as "police in a Western country do in the case of a known criminal," waiting until the person committed some misdemeanor, then using the derogatory information gathered earlier as supplementary evidence of accessory crimes.

Catholic priests and fundamentalist pastors who "emphasized the conflicts between religion and the world, or the thought of dying for one's religion" with texts taken from the Bible, could not be prohibited openly, since this was their legal right. ("This," said Hsiao Feng, "was a very difficult problem.") However, they were called to the Religious Affairs Bureau office to be "persuaded and educated." They were then warned that this was being recorded against them in their report.

In another confidential directive from Peking the different attitudes towards Catholics, Protestants, and fundamentalist sects were defined:

Catholics are more united, stricter and more conservative on the religious side, and are more obstinate and reactionary on the political side, than Protestants. The Protestants have many sects with many contradictions between them. Since they have such complicated divisions they are easier to control. Protestants can be divided into two large groups, those who are "social gospel" and those who are "fundamentalist" (spiritual). The former are enlightened, comparatively speaking, the latter are conservative and obstinate, and also opposed to the Three Self Movement.

The fundamentalist sects must receive more attention and stricter control. Pastors of these churches are more likely to become "objects of struggle" in any political movement. Fundamentalist standards depend largely on the inclination of their faith. Most of them believe in "the end of the world" and oppose other sects. The fundamentalist churches are Christian Assemblies (Little Flock), Evangelist Boat Mission, Ling Liang Evangelistic Mission, Baptists, Devotion Church (Ling Shou Hui), Assemblies of God etc.

In dealing with the social gospel groups cadres must emphasize social classes, first classifying each person according to his social class then dealing with him accordingly.

Hsiao Feng elaborated on the difference in approach to Catholic and Protestant, outlined in directives from Hsi Chung-hsün, the vice-director of the Central Propaganda Department.

From a political point of view both Catholicism and Protestantism are opposed to Communism. The Marxist-Leninist view of the world is materialistic; the material determines thought, therefore the material is of the first order and spirit is clearly second. But the world view of religions is idealist: the spirit shapes the material, so the spirit is of the first order. The Marxist duty is to establish a Communist society in the world without any exploitation, but Christianity wants people to bear the oppressions of the ruling class or escape from the struggle between classes to their illusory heaven in a mysterious universe.

The first Protestant foreign missionary to come to China to spread Christianity was Morrison, and he was able to come because of special privileges resulting from the Opium War of 1842, so he was a pioneer of the cultural aggregation of the Imperialists. Catholicism is a world religion. Wherever it is found it is under the control of the Vatican, and a small town of 800 inhabitants is a notorious anti-communist fort.

Hsiao Feng claimed that many intellectuals—scientists, writers, educators, doctors—who were "neutral in politics" did not agree with this interpretation of Christianity's contribution to China. They argued that in the fifth decade of the nineteenth century China's natural science was in a backward condition; that many of the foreign missionaries had been expert in medicine, astronomy, and mechanics, and with their religion they also brought Western science and civilization. Hsiao also claimed that several history books, although published under the Communist regime, admitted this contribution of Christianity.

Hsi Chung-hsün emphasized constantly that because of its political and historical background Catholicism was more opposed to communism than Protestantism was, and gave directions accordingly. He quoted every anti-Communist statement made from the Vatican, quoted prayers with anti-Communist content, and had translated into Chinese anti-Catholic pamphlets published in Russia. Two of these, were "Pope Pius the Twelfth" and "The Vatican—International Anti-Communist Fort."

The Protestant Christians, Hsi Chung-hsün affirmed, were more likely to follow the trends of the times. Their organization was "loose." There were so many complications that they should be treated separately; the best strategy was to divide them and win them over to communism. Their traditional differences became more obvious under Communist pressure, and they tended to disintegrate or to be absorbed into each other.

Catholicism and Protestantism were both anti-Communist, but they had different ways of dealing with communism. Catholics were reactionary and obstinate, Protestants crafty and cunning. They could be likened to practitioners of Chinese boxing. Catholics fought communism with the "Shao Lin" method, which calls for open striking on the important parts of an opponent's body. Protestants used the "Tai Chi" method, or using hidden or secret strength—internal exercises—to injure the opponent. Catholics openly opposed the Three-Self Movement, but Protestants superficially participated while trying secretly to upset it. "We, therefore, put work with Catholics at the head of our agenda in order definitely to put out the reactionary flame; but we must also be unceasingly alert toward the activities of Protestants."

The Communist Party insisted that every cadre engaged in united front work among the religions should constantly read the Bible, the Buddhist Sutras, Taoist doctrines, and the Koran so that they would have at least a working knowledge of these religions' basic principles, disciplines, and customs, as well as being alerted to ways in which Marxism-Leninism could be infused into their doctrines. After 1957 this tentative recommendation was made into an official qualification for prospective Religious Affairs cadres.

"Many a time my own attempt at 'infiltration' into religion almost ended in a joke," recounts Hsiao Feng. "I remember the time I was invited by the Canton Three-Self Patriotic Movement Committee to address students in a theological seminary. I quoted two passages from the Bible: 'But this I say, He which soweth sparingly shall reap also sparingly; and he which soweth bountifully shall reap also bountifully.' 'For even when we were with you, this we commanded you that if any would not work, neither should he eat.'[1]

"My purpose in doing so was to get them interested in reality and to emphasize the subject of patriotism. I also wanted to prove the correctness of the Marxist-Leninist theory, 'He who does no work will not eat,' from the viewpoint of Scripture, and bring their religious standpoint close to our political standpoint.

"However, some of the senior students asked me questions which I found difficult to answer, such as: 'Comrade Hsiao, will you please tell me whether in your opinion Jesus was a proletarian or not?'

"Of course, I could not give him a definite answer, for a materialist must never agree with an idealist. But I realized that he had asked the question without malice, and I was in some embarrassment. Finally I said that we could not escape the fact that the Bible contains many philosophical theories which are of benefit to real life, just as we cannot deny the fact that there exists a fundamental difference between the Bible and Marxism-Leninism. From the historical viewpoint we can find the name of Jesus in our book all right, but there is not enough material there for us to learn much about him.

"The necessity of infiltration of religion with Marxism-Leninism is based on the need 'to unify the religious circles and win them over to our side.' This involves reforming and using religion. The

result is often more confusion all round than anything else. The
more we attempted to put this policy into effect, the more we realized
that in the new Chinese society Christianity could not take the
place of Marxism-Leninism, nor could the latter take the place of
the former. As to which will eventually triumph," Hsiao concluded
thoughtfully and surprisingly, "it is difficult to say at this point."

In the meantime the significant factor emerging from obeying the
Party directive was that the Three-Self Patriotic Movement was
becoming every month more like any secular arm of the Communist organization. By 1958 the emphasis of the Three-Self Patriotic
Movement was no longer "self-government, self-support, self-propagation." These were "political" issues and already considered
"settled" by the government. The Three-Self Patriotic Movement
had been so altered that its main purpose was to organize all priests
and pastors to acquire "political and current affairs learning" and
to have every church activity completely fulfill the demands of government policy and law.

Ironically, Hsiao Feng claimed that he was often pressed into
solving internal problems in Protestant churches even after he had
expressed reluctance to do so. Sometimes he would be asked by
church leaders to appoint a pastor, or even to help a pastor examine a candidate for baptism. And he added, contemptuously, that
well-known church leaders willingly submitted to directives issued
over the telephone by obscure lower cadres of government.

But the chief method used by the Communists in "secularizing"
the Christian churches was by "hidden strength" operatives with
"single string connections." Hsiao Feng was in charge of religious
affairs in his area for some years before he even knew of this
Communist unit's existence. The operatives were specially selected "underground" Communist Party members from capitalist organizations, democratic parties, minority nationalities and religious
groups, who could use their Party-permitted acceptability and connection with these people to infiltrate the churches; hence "hidden
strength." These operatives were directly under the control of the
Communist Party, attached only to the director of the local United
Front Work Department, and had no contact with any other department or person. This was called "single-string connection," and
was accepted practice in Communist Party procedures for underground or infiltrating work.

The method was first used when the Communists came into power, and they began placing their people in mission schools and other organizations. Later they extended their activities to professional church workers. In 1954 the Central Committee officially announced to the Religious Affairs divisions in all provinces and cities that their work was being expanded. Each division should seek out reliable and influential persons in churches who might, after strict tests, be absorbed into this organization. Great importance was attached by the Central Committee to the work and the kind of person selected. It was pointed out that most of the Eastern Church leaders in Russia were actually Communist Party members, so that although the churches were still open and congregations worshiping, their understood purpose was propaganda for world peace and communism instead of religion.

The task of these selected "hidden strength" operatives was not just to collect information and win others, but to train themselves to manage a church or organization and gradually take the place of older pastors and leaders.

The "hidden strength" operatives were different from the usual Public Security Department workers. These were of two kinds: (1), members of churches who had committed crimes and were therefore subject to imprisonment: if such a person was willing to spy in the church he might be given a slight sentence or "excused from direct control"; (2) those who had been members of the Kuomintang or other reactionary organizations, or had worked in military, government, police, or military police before the "liberation." All such persons were intimidated and forced to supply information to the Public Security Department. They were known as "contrarily used persons" or "enemies used to work for you." They were directly under the control of the First Division of the Public Security Bureau, and used their positions as pastors or laymen to engage in spying, receiving no pay but official promises to "achieve merits to redeem crimes."

In each political campaign against religious workers or church members these "materials" were used by Public Security Departments to influence public opinion. The "contrarily used persons" who had no knowledge of law, and in any case were extremely frightened, usually exaggerated certain facts in order to achieve merit and redeem their crimes. For instance, in the period of the "tranquilize hidden counterrevolutionaries movement" in 1955, there were many cases in which these informers openly acknowledged that they had made mistakes and had persons wrongly arrested. In these instances the leading figures had to be released.

Hsiao Feng recalled that he had made a statistical survey of the number of churches and their members in Canton in 1952, with their monthly increase or decrease, and that the graph showed fifty-two churches and about seven thousand members. This was a decline of about one thousand church members since 1951, when there had been a sudden increase caused by the Korean War propaganda and "cadre examination movement." But in late 1952 during the "three-anti movement" (anti-avarice, anti-extravagance, anti-bureaucracy) the number of church members increased markedly by at least four hundred.

Hsiao Feng's explanation was that while many church leaders and members were persecuted, imprisoned, "struggled with," committed suicide or fled, many others became committed Christians or were baptized "in order to obtain some spiritual sympathy or comfort." He gave the example of a visiting group of preachers from Peking Christian Assembly (Little Flock) who came to Canton and joined with a group of Assembly of God Christians. Within a short time they opened another church, and during the period of the "three-anti movement" they had expanded from seventeen members to over two hundred. "Most of these were intellectuals—university instructors, teachers from primary and middle schools, university students, and even one military officer."

Other statistics recalled by Hsiao Feng were that "in those municipalities directly controlled by central and provincial governments alone, religious rightists averaged about fifteen in each city." Most of these were well-known Catholic priests or Protestant pastors, such as Catholic Bishop Tun Yi-ming, (whose trial as a counterrevolutionary in Kwangchow so upset the Vatican); and fundamentalist pastor Chow Liu Hsien-kao, arrested in 1955 as a counterrevolutionary, released, arrested again in the "anti-rightist" period later, and finally sentenced to twenty-five years' imprisonment.

But with the exception of such individuals, the policy of infiltration and secularization had been very successful. The Peking Union Theological Seminary was said to be free of government control, but was in fact run by influential Party members; most of the students were government-selected and expected to carry out the government policy. There was a smaller proportion of Party members in Nanking Theological Seminary, but the policy was the same and the results could be seen in the diminishing number of applicants for the university. The Union Theological Seminary in Canton was closed down in 1960 because of a shortage of personnel.

In their religious teaching the new "hidden strength" graduates opposed "supernatural sermons," especially the "final judgment" of Catholicism, and the "second coming of Christ" and "the last days of the world" of Protestantism. The influential Christian Assemblies were ordered "to abolish women's meetings, weekly breaking of bread [communion], personal interviews with church members before breaking of bread, and the rule against women speaking in church." All men and women were equal in the New China; and all Christians were expected to preach world peace, patriotism, love of the people, and "support for the actual world."

In 1957 Hsiao Feng's mother came from Hong Kong to visit him and other members of the family; while there she pleaded with him to go to Hong Kong. At that time, although he was having some personal conflicts in the department, he had no intention of leaving the country. But during the "anti-rightists" campaign in 1957 and afterward, he began to have increasing doubts about certain aspects of the Communist government's policy, and more inhibitions in implementing that policy in his own work. He knew that there would be no second chance for him if he ever slipped again. But even with all his caution, after a three-month period of self-criticism sessions in 1958 when everyone had to "bare their thoughts," he was accused of "rightist tendencies" and demoted "one grade." He was sent to a farm outside Canton for errant Party cadres to insure their ideological reeducation. At the farm he was subjected to the "three-eight system"—eight hours of physical labor, eight hours of political study, and eight hours of rest. During his time there he became friendly with someone in the hospital; with his help he feigned heart trouble, which gave him less labor and more leisure time. He devoted himself to writing, mostly novels and some poetry, and was able to keep out of controversial situations which might have proved fatal.

By this time, too, he had decided to take his mother's advice and join her in Hong Kong. The opportunity came during the "great exodus," and he was one of the many who crossed over into Hong Kong in 1962.

Hsiao Feng probably could now be classed as a "socialist." He has no religious affiliations, but a marked respect for the many who suffered for their faith during his tenure of office. He is contemptuous of those in all religions who were prepared to compromise as soon as some threat was waved at them, and then claimed that their frightened compromise was really in the interests of their fellow members or their religion. Sitting in Hong Kong, quiet, intelligent, and thoughtful, he remarked: "My own experience indicates that religion has an immeasurable power over one's life. Roman Empire domination cannot possibly destroy religion—it only makes people's devotion increase. During the land reform movement all the Catholic and Protestant churches in cities, towns, and villages were closed, but 'underground' congregations still existed. I wonder if it is not possible that in the future the 'home congregation' will be the most developed style of religious life. There are people of all faiths who, because of political treatment or economic difficulty or other problems, hide their ceremony of faith deeply in their hearts and never worship in public again."

This was a Communist Party worker's personal view of the spectacular drama being unfolded on the stage of China from 1949 onward, as an ancient faith and a modern ideology met head on in a monumental struggle. These twenty years will be a historic landmark for future historians, both secular and religious. But they are also of supreme importance to twentieth-century Christians throughout the world, for in these twenty years men and methods were tested in an unparalleled crucible of circumstances.

CHAPTER TWO

The Christian Contribution in China

THE EXACT TIME when Christianity entered China is not known. It is tempting to accept the legend that one of the twelve apostles, St. Thomas, was the first to bring the teachings of Jesus Christ to such an influential people and country. But there seems to be little doubt among modern scholars that this is merely "legend."[1]

Another well-known legend is that Emperor Ming of the later Han dynasty (A.D. 67) had a dream which led him to send messengers to the West in search for a new faith. Some Buddhist scholars believe that Buddhism was introduced into China by two Buddhists who came to China in response to Emperor Ming's search; but Christians who accept the story claim that the two messengers were not Buddhists but Christians from Central Asia, disciples of St. Thomas. The difficulty is that the story originated in the latter part of the second century and has no historical foundation.[2]

The first certain date concerning the entry of Christianity into China is connected with the work of the Nestorian Church during the T'ang dynasty (A.D. 618-907). It is taken from the Nestorian Monument erected at Hsianfu in A.D. 781, giving the date of arrival of Nestorian missionaries at Hsianfu, then the capital of China, as A.D. 635.

The Nestorian Monument was discovered in 1625 when some workmen uncovered a great slab of stone buried several feet under the ground near the district city of Chou-chih, thirty or forty miles southwest of Hsianfu in Shensi Province.[3] Latourette says that no ancient inscription is better known in the West, rubbings and models of the stone having been taken to many places in Europe and America for further studies. Although at first suspected as a possible pious fraud, it is now accepted as genuine.[4]

According to the text on the monument, Christianity was introduced by a Nestorian missionary called Alopen. The record begins with a statement of Christian doctrine, followed by an account of the Apostolic Age, the arrival of the first Christians in China, the fortunes of the infant Christian church there up to the erection of the stone, and finally a kind of eulogy, or recapitulation of the history in verse.

The history may be summarized as follows: In the year 635 Alopen, coming overland from the West from a country named Tachin (suggested as "Syria") arrived in the capital of China. The Emperor, T'ai Tsung, paid him great honor, sending one of his chief ministers to receive him. Alopen was brought to the palace, and there the Christian books were translated. After reading them Emperor T'ai Tsung promulgated a decree in 638 commanding a church and a monastery to be built in the capital. He also gave to Alopen and his followers the right to propagate their faith.

During the next two centuries the Christians experienced mixed fortunes. Under the vigorous but infamous Empress Dowager Wu, in 698-99, Christians were persecuted at the instigation of the Buddhists. Then there was a favorable period. But in A.D. 845 the Emperor Wu Tsung, who was an ardent Taoist, issued an edict prescribing Buddhism, condemned 4,600 monasteries to be destroyed, and ordered 300 foreign priests "to return to secular life, to the end that the customs of the empire may be uniform."[5]

By the end of the tenth century Nestorian Christianity had disappeared from China.[6] A combination of militant Mohammedan expansion and absorption by a tolerant Buddhism seems to have

been the reason for the disappearance of that early Christianity.
Mohammed died in A.D. 632 and the first impact of his terrifying
proselytising followers was on the Syriac region from which Alopen
had come. As the followers of Mohammed spread rapidly throughout three continents, the Nestorian Church, which had begun as "a
church on fire" but which had lost most of its early impetus in the
intervening centuries, crumpled before the onslaught of the rival
religion and, in China, was finally overrun.

The absorption of Christianity by Buddhism was more interesting,
and still presents an intriguing problem to scholars: Did early
Nestorian Christianity influence Buddhism, or did Buddhism influence and finally absorb Christianity?

Christianity had several things in common with the earlier religions of China. Like Buddhism and Confucianism, it put great
emphasis on ethics. Confucianism preached obedience to the ideal
of a distant past. Buddhism promised Nirvana to the individual
believer but saw the world as "illusory" and evil. Many of the
virtues held important by the Buddha and Confucius were also
stressed by Christians, and all worked for a perfect individual. Con-
fucian concern for an ideal social order and Jesus' teaching about
the Kingdom of God had many similarities. The idea of vicarious
suffering and of salvation by faith in the one who has so suffered is
to be found in Mahayana Buddhism as well as in Christianity. The
ritual of Mahayana Buddhism as practiced in Tibet is strikingly
similar to Roman Catholic practices. For instance, the same number
of days (forty-nine) as the minimum time spent in *bardo,* the
Mahayana equivalent of purgatory, would seem to indicate the influence of early Christian practices.

Kenneth Scott Latourette has written regarding this:

Much that is distinctive of the Nestorian, Russian Orthodox, and
Roman Catholic Churches bears a striking resemblance to Mahayana
Buddhism. All have monastic communities with attendant ascetic ideals.
All have elaborate rituals. Christian saints have a likeness to bodhisattvas.
*To the Chinese these three Churches do not come, then, as entirely
strange* [italics mine]. There is even the danger that because of the
resemblances the Chinese may identify the ideas derived from Buddhism
with the apparently similar but really different teachings of the Church.[7]

I have italicized the sentence above to indicate how, although

there was a gap of some six centuries between the disappearance
of early Christianity and its later reappearance, it was not "entirely
strange" or wholly foreign to the later Chinese. For when Christianity was reintroduced to China, it was in the Roman Catholic form.

Strictly speaking, there had been several missionary attempts by
Roman Catholics to "evangelize" China in the intervening centuries,
but it was not until the sixteenth century and the arrival of Francis
Xavier that Christianity began once again to make a considerable
impression on China. This period of Roman Catholic effort syn-
chronized with the Renaissance and Reformation movements in
Europe and the great exploratory ventures that were to influence
profoundly the whole world.

When Ignatius, the "General" of the new order called the Society
of Jesus, commanded one of the founder-members, Francis Xavier,
to set sail for the conversion of India, the Roman Catholic Church
had to seek material aid from Portugal. The only way to reach
India in 1541 was by Portuguese ship because only the Portuguese
had knowledge of routes, winds, currents, etc., and they kept their
knowledge a closely guarded secret. As a result, the church's missions in the East were linked with the power of Portugal; its rulers
claimed the right to appoint bishops, a claim which in later years
seriously affected the progress of the Church in Asia. The story of
Francis Xavier's labor in India, his mission to Japan, and his death
off the coast of China is a fascinating record of inspiring spiritual
zeal and depressing human failings.

In 1560 the Portuguese took Macao, and in 1574 Father Alex-
ander Valignano, Superintendent of the Jesuits' Missions to the
East, settled there. The words regarding China so frequently
ascribed to Francis Xavier—"Oh, rock, rock, rock, when wilt thou
open to my Lord!"—were really uttered by Valignano. He was the
one who selected and sent Fathers Michele Ruggieri and Matheo
Ricci in a "new approach" to introduce Christianity to China. He
wrote to the General of the Society of Jesus: "The only possible
way to penetration will be completely different from that which has
been adopted up to now in all the other missions in these countries."[8]

This "new approach" was to influence the whole Christian commitment, both Roman Catholic and Protestant, for the next four
centuries. Father Valignano maintained that the Chinese respect for

learning and their readiness to listen to anything that was put to them in an intelligent way, rather than as the religion of a civilization which claimed superiority to their own, would more readily open their minds to the acceptance of Christianity. Therefore, he gave instructions that all who were assigned to missionary work in China must as a necessary preliminary learn to read, write, and speak Chinese and acquaint themselves thoroughly with Chinese literature and Chinese manners and customs.

In 1582 Father Ricci succeeded in entering China, via Canton, and began his work in the city of Chao-ch'ing. His own account of the methods used so successfully are illuminating and significant:

The Fathers had hung up in their hall a map of the whole world, with the names in Arabic characters. When the Chinese understood what it was, never having seen or imagined such a thing before, all the more serious minded of them wanted to see it printed with Chinese characters so as to understand its contents better. . . . So the Father (i.e. Matheo Ricci, who wrote always in the third person) who knew something of mathematics, having been a disciple of Father Christopher Claver [friend and associate of Kepler and Galileo] when in Rome, set about the task, helped by one of the *literati,* a friend of his; and before long he had made a map of the world, bigger than the one in the house. . . . And it was the best and most useful work that could be done at that time, to dispose the Chinese, to give credit to the things of the Faith. For, up to then, the Chinese had printed many maps of the world with titles such as 'Description of the whole world' in which China was all, occupying the field with its fifteen provinces, and round the edge they depicted a little sea where a few islets were dotted about, on which they wrote the names of all the Kingdoms of which they had ever heard; and these all put together would not have equalled in size one of the provinces of China. . . . When they saw the world so large and China in a corner of it, so small to their way of thinking, the more ignorant began to make fun of such a description, but the more intelligent, seeing such an orderly arrangement of parallel lines of latitude and longitude . . . could not resist believing the whole thing true . . . it was printed again and again and all China was flooded with copies.

In the printed map China was put in the middle, but in its proportionate size. Ricci did not wish to hurt the feelings of the Chinese unnecessarily. His commentary continues further on:

Many were drawn by the big clock and the little one; others by the fine oil paintings and other prints; others by the various mathematical instruments, the maps of the world and the manufactured articles which came from Europe.

The books also made them all marvel on account of their different bindings with much gold and other ornamentation, besides the books on Geography and Architecture in which they could see so many countries and provinces all over the earth, the beautiful and celebrated cities of Europe and elsewhere, the great buildings, palaces, towers, theatres, bridges and churches. Later, musical instruments arrived which were much to their taste . . . very gradually they came to realize that our country, our savants, our people, were quite different from what up to that time they had thought all foreign countries to be, namely, barbarous and in no way comparable to their own.

On such occasions the Father began to speak of our Holy Faith. Consequently, the house was full all day of grave personages and the street full of their litters, the river bank in front of our house full of boats belonging to the mandarins. . . .[9]

I have quoted from Father Ricci at some length partly because of the importance of the manner in which Christianity was reintroduced into China but mostly because this became the standard approach of both Roman Catholics and Protestants in later centuries—Christianity was identified with the learning, techniques and material benefits of the West.

Ricci soon decided that the only way in which the whole Christian missionary venture to China could be placed on a secure base was to obtain the recognition of the Emperor. Otherwise the project could be endangered at any moment if some official reported the presence of strangers in the Empire. To obtain this recognition, the Father had to get to Peking. In order to make themselves acceptable to the Chinese *literati* en route, he and the other Fathers decided to grow beards and long hair (to distinguish them from the poorly regarded Chinese monks, or bonzes) and to wear the distinctive dress of Chinese scholars.

Ricci arrived in Peking in 1601, just twenty-one years after landing in Macao. During the intervening period missions had been set up in several places along the way. When Ricci died in 1610, an imperial edict ordered a monument to be erected to his memory. His greatest monument, however, consisted of about 340 works on religion, philosophy, and mathematics which he and his colleagues had published in support of the second stage of their new approach: by showing the Chinese how wrong they were in purely material matters, to help them see how wrong they must be in spiritual teaching. By 1670 there were approximately one hundred thousand Christians in China, and approximately ten thousand were being converted every year.[10]

Unfortunately, about this time groups of Dominicans and Franciscans had begun to arrive in China; but they were not welcomed by the Jesuits, and a bitter controversy arose between them. Under the Manchu Emperor Kang-hsi (1669-1722) the Jesuits enjoyed unparalled imperial favor. But a difference of opinion among Dominicans, Franciscans, and Jesuits over the translation of "God," and over the true significance of ancestor worship brought the emperor and the pope into direct conflict. The emperor, angered that any foreigner should dare to express an opinion on Chinese practices, issued a decree: "Henceforth no European missionary will be permitted to spread his religion in China. Thus we shall avoid further trouble."[11] With Kang-hsi's death in 1722 there began the decline of the great Christian experiment which was to last until the opening years of the nineteenth century. A combination of factors—persecution in China, the overbearing attitude of the Portuguese traders at Macao, the haughty conduct of the East India Company at Canton, and the overthrow of the papacy by Napoleon Bonaparte in 1809—combined to accelerate the decline of Christian witness in and missions to China. At the beginning of the eighteenth century there were some three hundred thousand Christians in China; by the end of the century there were barely two hundred thousand.

It was in the nineteenth century that Protestant Christianity awoke to the necessity of spreading their faith. In 1800 there was not a single Protestant Christian living in China. In 1853 there were 350 Protestant communicants; and by 1889 there were 37,289.[12] There were several reasons for this phenomenal increase.

At the outset of the nineteenth century the Chinese were firmly determined to keep aloof from all contact with the increasingly encroaching Western countries. They refused diplomatic relations on equal terms and permitted foreign trade through only one port, Canton, and on conditions that were galling to the Westerners. The ruling Ch'ing dynasty, composed of descendants of the Manchus who had conquered the country in the seventeenth century, had deteriorated. They were incapable of providing the kind of leadership required to guide China through the revolutionary currents flooding in from the West.

To the north and northwest Russia had extracted from China several treaties by which she annexed some 3,250,000 square kilometers of former Chinese territory.[13] Two wars with Great Britain (the ostensible cause was resistance to the importing of opium, but the primary cause was the unwillingness of Britain to accept the conditions of trade imposed by China) produced more treaties which gave the British Hong Kong, opened numerous ports for foreign residence and commerce, allowed foreigners to travel anywhere in the Chinese Empire, provided for diplomatic exchange on the basis of equality, and—most important, from the Christian missions standpoint—conceded to missionaries the privilege of teaching the Christian faith and guaranteed permission to Chinese to become Christians.

Dr. Robert Morrison was the first Protestant missionary of the London Missionary Society. He came to China in 1807 and became an interpreter of the East India Company in order to have a secure position. Like Ricci, he studied the Chinese language and almost single-handedly compiled a Chinese dictionary, supervised the establishment of the Anglo-Chinese College at Malacca, and translated the Bible into the book language of China. When he died in 1834, there were ten converts.

Until 1856, at the end of the second war against China, Protestant missionaries worked in the treaty ports. They ventured inland only on short excursions of twenty to thirty miles. This continued until 1860.

American missionaries outnumbered English by two to one. The explanation for this difference lay primarily in the fact that the United States had opposed the opium trade, and therefore the Chinese felt they had more right to teach the moral law than the English. In 1845 there were twenty American male Protestants in China, ten English and one German. Ten years later there were twenty-four English and forty-six Americans.[14]

Yet, as Latourette observed, "In spite of the community of interest and purpose among Protestants little attempt was made to approach China unitedly." However, in the matter of translating the Bible, there was some measure of cooperation.[15]

The London Missionary Society was soon joined by the American Board of Commissioners for Foreign Missions, followed by the American Presbyterians, the Protestant Episcopal Church of the United States, the American Baptists, and the American Methodists. In 1853 James Hudson Taylor of the Chinese Evangelisation Society—later to be the founder of the China Inland Mission—arrived in China. He became sick, went back home, finished his study of medicine, and returned to China, to become one of its most significant Christian missionary figures.

All of these societies occupied themselves with the production and dissemination of literature—Bible portions and gospel booklets—and with setting up educational establishments and medical centers.

Hudson Taylor had set himself systematically to accomplish the "evangelism of China" by recruiting more and more missionaries to go into the interior of China to "preach the gospel." In 1865 he founded the China Inland Mission, and issued a call for twenty-four workers, two for each of China's twelve inland provinces. In 1886 he called for one hundred missionaries. Finally, for one thousand. They all came—and more. When he died in 1905, there were almost one thousand in the China Inland Mission.

But a man of different approach was Dr. Timothy Richard. He was converted in a Welsh revival meeting and came to China in 1870 with the English Baptist Missionary Society. The great famine of 1877-79 in Shansi was in a sense a turning point for him. He saw that Western knowledge was needed, as well as the gospel, in order to deal with such economic disasters and to raise the standard of living. In his diary at that time he noted:

Heard stories at the inn that night of parents exchanging their children as they could not eat their own, that one dared not go to the pits for coal as mules, donkeys, and their owners were liable to be killed and eaten . . . I heard from other eye-witnesses that they had seen 270 dead on the roadside in three days . . . small wonder that I began to doubt my senses or my sanity, amid such scenes of horror. Was I among the living or the tormented dead?[16]

Richard was one of the few who made the attempt to cross the great gulf between Protestants and Roman Catholics in China. He gives his own account of an incident provoked by the governor of Shansi Province:

[The Governor's] brother, Tseng Kwoh Fan, the most eminent statesman in China during the Taiping rebellion, had already presented his views on Roman Catholicism and Protestantism to the Government to the effect that these two parties hated each other so much that they would counteract each other's influence and thus save the Chinese Government any aggressive action against either. When I asked the Governor's advice as to how I should best dispose of the sums I might in future receive for famine relief, he replied, with a twinkle in his eye: "There is a Roman Catholic missionary in this city who applied a few days ago for some grain for an Orphanage in his charge. You had better hand over your two thousand taels to him." I thanked him for his suggestion, and replied that I would call on the Bishop to discuss the matter with him. . . . The Bishop, however, would not agree to my proposal.[17]

Richard became secretary of the Society for the Diffusion of Christian and General Knowledge in 1891; he founded the first public school for Chinese in Shanghai, and after the Boxer Rebellion helped to found the university at T'aiyuanfu in Shansi. His aim was to try to reach the "official class." The Chinese had suffered unbelievable military defeats and diplomatic humiliations at the hands of the Western powers, and many were anxious to find out the "secret" of the strength of the Western nations. Richard took this opportunity to associate with the ruling class—leading liberals and officials—in order to better help the poor.

To summarize the period: During the eighteen years between the Treaty of Nanking and the Peking Convention, some seventeen missionary societies had started work in China. Some 160 to 170 workers were sent out, not counting wives.[18] By 1914, according to the *China Mission Year Book, 1915,* Protestant missionaries numbered 5,462.[19]

In his *Christianity in a Revolutionary Age,* Vol. III, Kenneth Scott Latourette presents an excellent summary of the period.[20] All Protestant missions stressed education, even those with a more evangelistic emphasis like the China Inland Mission. These schools were the main sources of Western learning, although until the Chinese civil service examinations were abolished in 1905 they were not very important, because they did not equip students with traditional Chinese learning. After 1905, however, the demand for Western learning was high and the schools grew accordingly.

Protestants tended to concentrate on higher education—secondary schools and colleges—rather than on elementary education which the Roman Catholics stressed. Denominations tended to join the support of these schools, particularly colleges and universities, and to place them strategically.

Protestants also brought Western medical practice and knowledge to China. Many Protestant mission stations had a hospital or dispensary as part of the ministry, and eventually set up medical and nursing schools with the most advanced knowledge available. By 1914 several medical schools had been established.

Latourette lists other benefits instituted by Protestants in response to needs: "units of the Red Cross, public playgrounds, social service clubs, labour-saving machinery in the spinning of cotton, and methods for improving the quality of silk-worm eggs. They fought the age-old custom of binding the feet of women, combatted the production, sale, and use of opium . . . sought to ameliorate the lot of the blind, the deaf, and the dumb," founded orphanages, gave famine relief, encouraged sports and physical education.

By the end of the nineteenth century the Protestant communicants were said to number 80,682. In 1915 there were 268,652 communicants, 62,274 baptized noncommunicants, and 190,958 others under instruction. The Protestant community totaled 526,108. At the same time the missionaries were beginning to recruit and educate a Chinese clergy and to bring the Chinese churches to the point where they would be self-governing, self-supporting, and self-propagating.

But the proliferation of denominations, both outside and inside the missionary societies, created dissensions and problems. In addition to combined educational and medical work, other forms of cooperation were tried, such as the Christian Endeavour movement and the Young Men's and Young Women's Christian Associations, or even unions of branches of the same denomination from different countries.[21] The arrangement which was to have the most significant effect, however, was the "comity agreements." These perpetuated the divisions of denominationalism by dividing the country into areas where each denomination could carry out its practices without interference from others.

While the Protestant missions were spreading and consolidating rapidly, the Roman Catholics had been slow in returning to the country where earlier they had had such an important impact. There were several reasons for this lag. Napoleon had broken up the papacy, the earlier missionaries had come from Europe, and the Industrial Revolution and the rise of Great Britain and America to wealth had outstripped these other nations.

The rise of France and the French joint venture with Britain in the second war against China gave the Roman Catholics a new opportunity and fresh impetus to reintroduce their faith into China. In order to understand the legal basis upon which the French founded their right to support their missionaries in China, and the many bitter conflicts which arose later between Roman Catholics and the Chinese government, it will be useful to give some of the important excerpts from the treaties and conventions.

In the Whampoa Treaty of 1842 between France and China the twenty-second article reads:

. . . The French may also in the same manner set up churches, hospitals, hospices, schools and cemeteries. For this purpose, the local authority, after having agreed with the consul, shall designate the districts which are most suitable for the French residence and the places where the aforesaid building operations may be constructed. . . .

If any Chinese violate or destroy churches or French cemeteries those responsible should be punished according to the severest laws of the country.[22]

The second war with China ended in 1858 with the signing of the Treaty of Tientsin. The thirteenth article of the treaty reads:

The Christian religion having as its essential purpose the leading of men to virtue, the members of all the Christian communions shall enjoy entire security in regard to their persons, their property and the free exercise of their religious practices, and an effective protection shall be granted to the missionaries who go peacefully through the interior of the country, provided with regular passports, of which there has been mention in art. 8. . . .

No hindrance shall be put in the way, by the authorities of the Chinese Empire, of the acknowledged right of any person in China to embrace Christianity if he wishes and to practice its tenets, without being liable to any penalty imposed for so doing.

Everything which has been previously written, proclaimed or published in China by order of the Government against the Christian religion is completely abrogated and is a dead letter in all the provinces of China.

Following the capture of Peking in 1860, a convention was signed. The sixth article stated:

In conformity with the imperial decree issued by the august Emperor, Tao-kuang, on 20th March, 1846, religious and charitable institutions which have been confiscated from the Christians during the persecutions of which they have been victims shall be restored to their owners through the mediation of His Excellency the Minister of France in China, to whom the Imperial Government will hand them over, together with the cemeteries and other buildings which depend upon them.

Through these provisions and others in a later treaty, only missionaries (and mostly Roman Catholics because of their earlier missionary effort) of all foreigners were able to own land in the interior of China outside the Treaty Ports. This factor was to have far-reaching implications for Christian witness in the years ahead.

The Jesuit missionaries under the new treaty's provision requested the return of the Catholic property in Shanghai where there had been an influential Catholic community, and by 1850 there were 70,000 Catholic converts. The first Catholic nuns, the Sisters of St. Paul, arrived in 1846. In 1855 the first Chinese sisterhood, the Congregation of the Presentation, was inaugurated outside Shanghai, at Zikawei, and in 1858 the Chinese Sisters of the Immaculate Heart of Mary were established in Manchuria. By the end of the nineteenth century there were 532,448 Catholics, 409 Chinese priests, and 759 Catholic foreign missionaries in China.

At the beginning of the twentieth century Christianity—at least in its educational, medical and literary aspects—had made a formidable cultural impact on China, as the following three tables will show:[23]

TABLE 1
COMPARATIVE TABLE OF CHINA MISSIONS
Showing Progress of Missions as reported at Conferences of
1877, 1890, and 1907

	1877	1890	1907
Protestant Missionaries	473	1,296	3,719
Chinese Helpers	750	1,657	9,998
Communicants	13,035	37,287	154,142
Stations	91	?	706
Out-Stations	511	?	3,794
Organized Churches	312	522	. . . . .
Hospitals	16	61)	366
Dispensaries	24	44)	
Contributions of			
Native Church	$9,271	$36,884	. . . . .
Day Schools	15	. . . . .	2,139
Pupils in Day Schools	280 ⌉		42,738
Boarding and Higher	7 ⎪ Total		
Schools	⎱ Pupils		255
Students in These Schools	292 ⌋	16,836	10,227

TABLE 2
CLASS *A*: MOSTLY THE BEST ANCIENT JEWISH,
APOSTOLIC, MEDIEVAL, AND
REFORMATION LITERATURE

SUBJECT	ROMAN CATHOLIC	RELIGIOUS TRACT SOCIETY	EDUCA- TIONAL ASSOCIA- TION	DIFFU- SION SOCIETY
Biblical Works	3	67	2	10
Church History	7	1	1	9
Christian Biographies	16	9	0	11
Theological Works	35	9		10
Apologetic Works	28	4		10
Devotional Works	43	22		13
Church Rules	1	2		1
Tracts	124	398		60
	257	512	3	124

TABLE 3

CLASS *B*: MOSTLY THE BEST MODERN LITERATURE

SUBJECT	ROMAN CATHOLIC	RELIGIOUS TRACT SOCIETY	EDUCATIONAL ASSOCIATION	DIFFUSION SOCIETY	NATIVE TRANSLATION
Comparative Religion	—	—	—	5	—
Philosophy	1	—	2	13	40
Ethics	—	—	1	—	—
Psychology	2	—	1	1	—
Medicine	2	—	17	2	70
Astronomy	1	—	5	1	20
Geography	3	1	11	2	40
Geology	—	—	3	—	—
Mineralogy	—	—	3	1	—
Universal History	—	—	2	9	7
National History	—	—	5	7	83
General Biographies	1	—	—	11	—
Mathematics	3	1	15	2	70
Physics	5	—	21	5	—
Chemistry	—	—	10	—	—
Electricity	—	—	2	2	—
Mechanics	—	—	3	—	40
Government	—	—	1	4	60
Law	—	—	2	4	40
Education	12	2	19	17	—
Language	—	—	—	—	50
Economics	—	—	3	6	30
Industry	—	—	13	—	—
Commerce	—	—	—	2	—
Agriculture	—	—	—	1	—
Statistics	1	—	—	1	30
Maps, Travels, Poetry, etc.	6	16	40	33	130
Miscellaneous	5	32	3	10	340
Totals	42	52	182	139	1,050
Class *A* Totals	257	512	3	124	—
Grand Totals	299	564	185	263	1,050

This tremendous expansion of education, medicine, and literature met with resistance and antagonism, riots and persecutions. These arose principally from popular resentment, reinforced by the objections of the scholar class who had been reared on Confucianism, against the growing threat of Christianity to the historic Chinese culture. The most famous of these outbreaks was the Taiping Rebellion.

In 1833 a young Chinese, Hung Hsiü-chüan, received a Christian booklet from Dr. Robert Morrison's assistant, Liang A-fah. Hung was subject to cataleptic fits and visions. When he failed to obtain a degree after ten years' study he claimed to have a vision, compounded of existing politics and the Christian booklet material, which launched him on a crusade against idolatry and the reigning dynasty. He finally took to arms and proclaimed himself the "Heavenly King." The Taiping, or "Heavenly Peace," Rebellion at the beginning was inspired by much that was good—condemnation of opium-smoking, the keeping of the sabbath, the circulation of the Bible (the British and Foreign Bible Society printed one million copies of the New Testament in Chinese for distribution in anticipation of the movement's success[24])—but it swiftly degenerated into a cruel and devastating holocaust, sweeping the whole of China.

The most serious outbreak directed against the Roman Catholics took place in 1870 in Tientsin, although it was as much anti-French as anti-Catholic. After destroying an orphanage, the French consulate, the adjoining church, and several foreigners, the anti-Christian demonstrations broke out in other parts of China. In the Boxer uprising of 1900 the Roman Catholics also suffered seriously, one report showing five bishops, thirty-one other European clergy, nine European sisters and more than thirty thousand Chinese Catholics killed. There were even more Protestant casualties.[25]

The blame for these terrifying outbreaks did not lie in the message of Christianity or in the messengers, nor even in the social and cultural methods used. The problem was the close association of Christianity with the nineteenth-century expedient policies of the European powers, gathered like vultures around the dying body of China. With the defeat of China by Japan in 1894-95, there began a series of humiliations for China that were to have far-reaching repercussions in the twentieth century. The *coup d'état* of 1898; the assumption of official rank by the Roman Catholic missionaries in

1899; the seizure of Kiaochow by Germany because of the murder of two Roman Catholic missionaries; the Russian entry into Manchuria and the fortification of Port Arthur; the British occupation of Weihaiwei—these were but a few of the many demands, treaties and humiliating circumstances overwhelming China at the beginning of the twentieth century.

With the founding of the Republic of China in 1912 there was an acceleration of Christian activity throughout the country, greatly helped by the fact that Dr. Sun Yat-sen, the father of the republic, was a Christian. Later Chiang Kai-shek became a Christian as did his brothers-in-law T. V. Soong and H. H. Kung.

In 1918 there were 1,456 foreign Roman Catholic priests, 834 Chinese priests, and 1,963,639 converts. By 1926 there were more than 1,184 Chinese priests, or 41 percent of all priests in China, and in that same year six Chinese bishops were consecrated in Rome. There were then over 2,000,000 Roman Catholics in China. In 1941 Chinese Catholics numbered 3,313,398 with another 512,263 catechumens. The number of Chinese priests had risen to 2,186—still less than half the total number of priests in China. That year 82,338 adult catechumens were baptized into the Church.[26] The extent of Roman Catholic witness in China when the Communists took over is noted in Chapter Seven.

By 1935 there were 481,227 Protestant Christians in 6,310 organized local churches. There were 123 separate missionary organizations, and Chinese religious workers numbered 15,680. In 1922, 21 organizations with a membership of 300,000 joined the National Christian Conference. By 1927 an "indigenous" organization, the Church of Christ in China, had brought together most of the Protestant denominations. In 1935 it had 91,415 members; in 1949, 176,983.[27]

By 1937 there had been a sizable increase in the number of Chinese religious leaders. There were more than two thousand Chinese ordained pastors, and roughly two thousand laymen who were on the staffs of religious organizations. There were also about the same number of women workers. Foreigners on the staffs of these organizations were still nearly six thousand, the majority of whom were women—significant of the increasing part women were playing in Protestant institutions. The Chinese had numerical control not only of the National Christian Council but also of church schools and of the medical end of the work. They also controlled the Y.M.C.A. and the Y.W.C.A.[28]

The Roman Catholic writer, Columba Cary-Elwes, commenting on this rapid Sinification, expressed certain reservations:

> The sinification of the Protestant bodies in China was not in itself a bad thing. It would have been well if the Catholics had advanced along that road much faster also. But in the case of the Protestants there were peculiar dangers. The Protestant Chinese neophytes were undoubtedly zealous, but they were not so well grounded in their religion, so well instructed as the Catholics. . . . Thus, once the American or European direction was relaxed, the dogmatic allegiances relaxed also; and the tendencies were towards Modernism on the one hand, or to social work on the other. This latter tendency was to make it fatally easy for many Christians brought up in a philanthropic Christianity to drift in the direction of Communism, not realizing the theological implications of this new creed and its incompatibility with the true teachings of Christ.[29]

But while this Sinification of the Roman Catholic and subdivided Protestant Christian witness in China was taking place, a much more significant "grass-roots" movement had begun, which was "indigenous" in the true sense. This was, if I may define the term "indigenous," a spontaneous native version of Christianity based on New Testament principles rather than a national variety of imported Western ecclesiastical systems as represented by Roman Catholic and Protestant churches. What the latter were attempting to do was to superimpose Chinese nationals on Western-conceived ecclesiastical structures; while the former personified a complete break with later Western tradition and a return to first-century New Testament church principles and practices.

The most widespread of these churches was the "True Jesus Church" begun by Paul Wei in 1917. The "Little Flock," as they were popularly known (or "Christian Assemblies," as they were known among themselves), was begun by Watchman Nee in 1926. The "Jesus Family" was begun by Ching Tien-ying in 1921. The "China Jesus Independent Church" was begun in Shanghai in 1906 by Pastor Yu Kuo-chen; and the "China Christian Independent Church" was begun in Shantung in 1912. The Ling Liang, or "Spiritual Food" Church, was begun by Timothy Dzao, and the

"Spiritual Work" Church followed later, with many more splinter and smaller groups.[30]

Thus, whether in institutional or in evangelical work Christianity had woven itself into the fabric of China, from peasant to President, in a manner which the new revolutionary Communist leaders in Peking could never tolerate. As Latourette concluded:

Although in 1914 its adherents numbered only about one in two hundred of the population—a much smaller percentage than in India— Christianity was having a pronounced effect upon the revolution which, arising from the impact of the Occident, in that year was still in its early stages.[31]

CHAPTER THREE

1949—End of an Era

CHRISTIANITY IN CHINA in the 1930's, as the most "recent" of the religions of China, must have seemed an easy target to the chauvinistic Communists. Christianity carried the apparent standard stigmas of the Communist demagogue; i.e., it had come with imperial conquest, its missionaries had come in the same ships as opium, it had been expanded by hated treaties and gunboat threats.

In the period prior to the war with Japan, the Communists were openly hostile to Christian missions in China, and in the areas in which they operated they drove the missionaries away. After the temporary truce in 1937 between the Communists and the Kuomintang, however, active persecution ceased for some time.

From 1937 on the Communists agreed to work with Chiang Kaishek's Nationalists to fight their common enemy, the Japanese. The Communists were strong mainly in the northwest part of China, and after the defeat of Japan, they began to secure their own positions, to build up arms, and were threatening to march into Japanese-occupied territory in the north and northeast. Eventually Mao Tse-tung was persuaded to go to Chungking for talks with Chiang Kai-shek, but even then the two Chinese armies were beginning their civil war.

The two parties arranged a cease-fire and a fusion of the two armies in the first months of 1946, and a combination government. But the Communists did not wait for the new government to be set up. Their troops were still fighting and advancing toward Tientsin and Weihaiwei on the north coast south of Peking. When the Americans flew Chinese troops up to Peking to combat the Communists, the Communists retaliated by refusing to help set up the National Assembly which they had agreed on. Finally Chiang Kai-shek called for the whole of China to resist and subdue the rebellion.[1]

In the north the situation was ominous, both politically and from the point of view of Christianity. The invading Japanese army had been extremely hostile to Christian missionaries, classifying them as "enemy aliens," then interning them and taking over the mission stations. The situation at the time in regard to Catholics in the north was somewhat easier. Many of the Catholic missions were run by Spaniards, who were neutral, or by Italians, who were allies; so the Japanese left them alone. But when the Communists returned, they were hostile to the "neutral" missionaries and used the allegation of cooperating with the enemy to drive out almost all of the Catholic missions which had survived in northern China. By the end of the war the hostility of the Japanese to Protestant missionaries and the hostility of Communists to Catholic missionaries had removed most of the missions from the northern provinces. Missions in the large cities, however, were taken over from the Japanese by the Nationalists, and the many hundreds of foreign missionaries returning after the war were able to occupy these. South of the Yangtze River there was an ever greater influx of foreign missionaries returning to mission stations and educational institutions.[2]

In 1946, therefore, in both Catholic and Protestant circles there was considerable optimism regarding the future of Christianity in China. Chiang Kai-shek was a Christian, along with his brothers-in-law, and their influential wives, and such well-known figures as C. T. Wang, Wang Chung-hui, and Feng Yu-Hsiang.

Many evidences were claimed by Christian observers that China was more interested in Christianity than she had ever been. Nearly three million copies of the Scriptures were distributed by the Bible Society in one year, and the Bible was the best-selling Chinese book. Christian literature was in great demand. Work among university and high school students was successful and increasing. The China Inter-Varsity Fellowship held a summer conference in 1947 in Nanking which was attended by more than two hundred delegates from all over China.

The big city churches were always full, some of which held from one to three thousand people. More young people than ever were preparing for the ministry, and for the first time these included a good number of university graduates.[3]

But the close association of both Protestant and Catholic Christian witness with their Western governments and with the Nationalist government of Chiang Kai-shek was to provide a rude awakening and a catastrophic decline. The latter policy was particularly unfortunate for Christian witness because of the vast corruption at all levels of the Nationalist regime. The lack of moral fiber in the government was apparent, it seemed, to all but Christians. Or if Christians did see it, they could do little about it, and few Christian voices were raised against the increasing corrupt practices in high places. And when they were, little notice was paid by the government.[4] Most Protestant and Catholic leaders not only identified themselves with the Nationalist regime but went out of their way to thank God on public occasions for "Christian leadership."

C. P. Fitzgerald, the noted historian on China, has written:

The Catholics, however, under the general opposition to Communism which the Vatican had endorsed, tended to the support of the Nationalist cause. The leading members of the Chinese hierarchy were openly on the side of the Kuomintang. The foreign missionaries who, as among the Protestants, no longer occupied most of the higher posts, were also strongly anti-Communist, and, although not great admirers of the Kuomintang, still felt that from the point of religion it was the cause to back. Not all foreign Catholics agreed with this attitude; many would have preferred neutrality, but the church as a whole came to be regarded as one of the few non-governmental organizations which supported the Kuomintang. This did it great harm in the years that followed.[5]

The glaring anomaly was realized too late to correct, a conclusion reluctantly arrived at from an agonizing reappraisal several years after all foreign missionaries had been ordered out of China and had returned to their own countries.

Writing in 1953, the Rev. David Paton, who was "a Catholic Christian of the Anglican obedience" in China, records:

The main charges are now two:

That Christian missions and the Churches they have fostered have throughout presupposed and disseminated the capitalist culture of the West and have been allied with such forces in China as were sympathetic to or could be the tools of the capitalist and imperialist West; and therefore that objectively speaking the mission and the Church were fundamentally reactionary forces, opposed to the true interests of the people, and the hangers-on if not active agents of the interests of Western powers; and would remain so even if, as missions have for decades declared to be their ultimate aim, the mission were itself wound up and all missionaries retired leaving the Church wholly responsible.

Secondly, that whatever may have been the formal aim of missions, their actual policy was such as not to foster but to preclude the development of a genuinely dynamic, self-governing self-supporting and expanding Church.[6]

This tragic self-reproach was echoed by many other writers in other journals and mission reports.

Inside China the political confusion that existed from 1947 to 1949, bad as it was, was as nothing compared to the confusion in the sphere of missions. The ordinary missionary, Roman Catholic and Protestant, gave little or no thought to the cataclysm convulsing China. Getting on with their daily tasks of preaching, teaching, doctoring, or nursing, they left it to the leaders of their missions to make the policy decisions. These activities were carried on even as the Communists took Peking in February, 1949, and Nanking in April. Throughout the remainder of that year one after another of the leading cities fell, bringing the whole of China under Communist control.

There were considerable difficulties for the missionaries, of course, as all government administration collapsed with the defeat of the Nationalists and their flight to Formosa. There were no mail deliveries, shops were closed because of lack of goods or for fear of looting, banks were closed down as money lost all value, transport ground to a halt. All of these changes naturally limited the activities of missionaries, whatever their function; but within their schools, hospitals, churches, and compounds they tried as best they could to keep things going.

As Communist officials entered the cities, towns, and villages with the Communist armies, they introduced some semblance of order and reassured the people that the new regime would not interfere with religion.[7] Some missionaries began to leave, especially those with children; but both Protestant and Roman Catholic mission policy, generally speaking, was to keep the missionaries at their stations.

For several months after the Communist take-over, especially in the large cities, all went well, although in some of the remoter areas and smaller villages there were reports of churches being commandeered as garrisons for Communist troops. But more people were reported to be attending churches. Christian broadcasting continued. Students met freely and held Christian meetings in their schools and classrooms. Graduates from Bible schools left for the west and northwest of China to preach.[8]

Miss Helen Willis, who was in charge of the Christian Book Room, Shanghai, and who lived there until 1959, has recounted of those days:

So Shanghai was "liberated."

That first summer was a strange time. Business was almost at a standstill. We were cut off from the outside world. The once crowded harbor was almost empty, and the streets had not half their previous traffic. Yet daily life went on with not so many outward changes. For some reason the Communists did not interfere with life in Shanghai nearly so much or so soon as in smaller towns and in the country. People coming into the city from the interior would say: "Oh, you have not been properly liberated yet. You can still do what you like, you are almost free!" . . .

For four months we were almost entirely cut off from the outside world. Now and again people were able to get away by ships waiting at the mouth of the Yangtze; but no ships came in, and for four months there were no letters. . . .

A feeling of tension was kept up by the constant reports of mass arrests and executions; and almost daily one saw truckloads or jeeploads of wretched men and women, crouching on the floor, being hurried away to judgment.[9]

On June 30, 1950, a group of Christian leaders and missionaries was called together in Shanghai to hear the report of a meeting held in May in Peking between several church leaders and several high Communist officials, including Chou En-lai. This conference had lasted for a good part of three days and one night. Among the church leaders were Dr. Y. T. Wu, manager and editor of the Associated Press (Y.M.C.A.); Liu Liang-mo, secretary of the national Y.M.C.A.; the Reverend George Wu, general secretary of the National Christian Council; Cora Deng, secretary of the Y.W.C.A.; Ai Nien-san, a leading Lutheran; Methodist Bishop Z. T. Kaung; and Dr. T. C. Chao of Yenching University.[10]

These leaders had been responsible for a report circulated to Christian leaders and mission boards the previous December.[11] The report had given some indication of what was to follow and caused great concern. It read in part:

A new chapter in the history of China has begun; a new era has dawned. A new "People's Government" has been born under the leadership of the Chinese Communist Party with the cooperation of all the revolutionary elements in the country, and with the avowed common purpose of putting into execution the political, social and economic principles of the New Democracy. . . . From now on, a new political concept, a new philosophy, a new creed and a new mode of living will be instilled into the masses of the people with a vigor that is hitherto unknown. Much of China's traditional heritage will be rigorously scrutinized, and, if need be discarded; many new and far-reaching policies will be put into execution. Likewise, much of western culture that has been introduced in recent years will be re-examined and shorn of its undesirable elements. Out of this will be born a new China, radically different from the China of old. Compared with the present moment, the change of dynasties in the past four thousand years has little significance; the revolution of 1911 and 1927, and the war of resistance are but wavelets in the rapids of time. From such a change there is no turning, and at such a time a diehardness has no place.

Up to this time the Chinese churches had managed to keep themselves aloof from the political issues raging in the secular field. But a clash was certain, since the new regime had declared that all phases of life must necessarily come under the influence of politics. This was contrary to the traditional Protestant view of the separation of church and state. In the new era about to begin, political influences would permeate every aspect of the lives of the people. Chinese Christians were now faced as never before with their responsibilities as citizens in society as well as servants of God.

The report specifically stated three fundamental points of future policy: "(1) Policy determination and financial administration must be passed over to Chinese leadership. (2) Regarding missionaries, while there was nothing in principle to make the future position of the missionary untenable, his future contribution would lie 'in special service projects,' not in administrative matters. He would have to have 'an open mind' on political matters and become accustomed to an 'economical environment' on a level with the people, and travel would be restricted. (3) Mission funds without strings attached would be permitted to enter China temporarily, but the Chinese churches from henceforth would have to be responsible for their own support."

The May, 1950, meeting in Peking resulted in the publication of a document which came to be known as "The Christian Manifesto." It was published in July, 1950, under the title: "Direction of Endeavor for Chinese Christianity in the Construction of New China." (See Appendix I.) The manifesto appeared over the signature of forty of the outstanding Christian leaders of China, and the new government made it clear that it was the responsibility of every Christian leader to persuade others to sign the document and approve the policy.

Something of what this foreshadowed was contained in a covering letter to the manifesto (signed by the attending church leaders) which went out to Chinese Christian leaders, making some of the statements in the manifesto more explicit:

The Church must support the Common Platform, accept the leadership of the Government and work harmoniously with it. It must come to a clear understanding of the way American imperialism has used the church, and eradicate all the results of that imperialism. As a principle it must use no foreign funds and no foreign personnel, and on these two points, it must consult with the Government. During the period of Land Reform all church activities except routine Sunday services, prayer-meetings, etc., should cease.[12]

When this radical manifesto was published in all the daily newspapers on September 23, it carried 1,527 signatures of Christian leaders. Within a year or two 400,000, or about half the total Protestant membership of China had signed it.

In addition to its proclaimed general intention, the manifesto had several other noteworthy features. For instance, the admission (later suppressed) that "Protestant Christianity . . . has made a not unworthy contribution to Chinese society," the identification of Christianity with "imperialism,"[13] the subservient part which Chinese Christians had played in Christian churches and organizations, and the overt part which these leaders, churches, and organizations were to have in a political association with the new Communist regime.

The charge that Christian missions were a part of the imperialist aggression of the West could not be evaded. David Paton lists some of the evidence. In addition to the clauses in the unjust treaties giving missionaries the right to travel, to own property, and to preach the gospel in inland China, there were other as obvious examples. Church architecture was Western, and even imitation Gothic; ritual and services were straight interpretations; prayerbooks were often poor and literal translations; and the hymnbook in general use by the union church had only 62 original Chinese hymns out of 512, and 72 Chinese tunes. Missionaries tended to keep to a Western style and standard of living, though there were exceptions, and their Chinese colleagues who attained the educational and financial means to do so joined them. Chinese Christians were rated more for their grasp of the English language and Western culture than for their understanding of Chinese language and literature.[14]

There was no government edict officially expelling the foreign missionaries from China. (See Appendix II, for "Peking Edict" of December 29, 1950.) But there was pressure. Leslie Lyall, a member of the China Inland Mission, gives an eye-witness account:

As if by pre-arrangement the local Communist cadres called on the local church leaders to enquire their reaction [to the Manifesto].
"You agree, of course?"
"Yes!"
"Then why do you still welcome the presence and help of these foreign imperialist missionaries?" . . .
Sadly and fearfully, they sent delegations to see the missionaries.
"We deeply appreciate all you have done for us in the past. But times

have changed! In the New China it will be very difficult for us to work together" (an embarrassed pause). "Perhaps it would be better if you gave up your Bible class. It might even be best if you didn't come to church at all!"[15]

And so the great exodus began. Before the missionaries left their stations they had to hand over the deeds of all mission properties and the control of most of the educational, medical, and charitable institutions to the government. Before any missionary could get an exit visa, a notice had to appear in the local newspaper inviting anyone who had a claim against the missionary to file it immediately. A local person also had to agree to be a sponsor for each missionary who left, to guarantee their conduct in the future. Some were detained for public trials and imprisonment. The government thus took over all schools, orphanages and hospitals, but made no payment to the churches or missions for the property they confiscated. They did, however, leave the theological and Bible schools to the churches, as well as the Bible House, and other Christian publishing companies.[16]

The Roman Catholics had chosen to remain. There had been considerable publicity over the persecution and torture of Catholic missionaries in North China from 1945 to 1949:

The worst period of this time was the bloody winter of 1948-49. Mob trials took place in every village. The church of Chunghi-Siwantze (in Chahar) was burnt and the Christians massacred. In the province of Jehel, priests, religious, laity were dragged over the frozen roads and then died either from blows or from exposure.[17]

Rome, however, ordered that no Catholic priest was to leave his station unless forced to do so through old age or illness. During the lull of 1949-50, the Roman Catholics prepared for a later time of persecution and suppression by intense printing and distribution of books "which would provide the doctrine for the time when priests were once again hunted." Many priests and bishops and nuns "proletarianized" themselves by working at some trade—from farming and weaving to medicine and pharmacy.[18]

With the publication of the Christian Manifesto, the same procedures used by the Communist cadres against Protestant missionaries were used against Roman Catholics. Attempts were made to get Catholics to declare that Internuncio Riberi was a "lackey of imperialists," then to repudiate the Pope and to support the other accusations against "foreign doctrine," "Western theology," "cultural aggression." When lay committees of Catholics were formed, under "persuasion," to control the worship in the churches, foreign and Chinese priests refused to attend the churches, or, if forced to go, refused to join the priest in the prayers. It was obvious that a crisis was inevitable.

According to *The Times* (London, February, 1951) this crisis took place on a June Sunday in Chungking when the Catholic congregation was leaving the church after mass. The congregation coming out of church was met by a procession timed to arrive at the same time, and the Catholic faithful were forced to join the demonstrators. The cry was "Down with the imperialist Riberi—let the government expel him."

The rest of the incident was described by Cary-Elwes:[19]

By late afternoon the regime had staged another of its monster Szechuan demonstrations. . . . The day's schedule called for a final summing-up of the aims of the demonstration to be delivered to the many marchers by various "interested participants." It was then that Father John Tung, aged forty-five, electrified Chungking's "Progressive Catholics" and the city's officialdom.

Ascending the speaker's rostrum, he traced on himself the sign of the Cross, and began, as all sermons preached in Catholic Churches begin, with the words, "In the name of the Father and of the Son and of the Holy Ghost." Then in the stillness as of a church he continued . . . The point of what I wish to say is this: "I offer myself as a sacrificial victim to bring about an understanding between the Government and the Church." . . .

"It is those very people, who deny the existence of God and of the immortal soul, who do not recognize the Vicar of Jesus Christ on earth—the Holy Father—and the position of the Hierarchy in relation to the Catholic Church, who would claim that the 'Three independencies' [self-government, self-support and self propagation] programme is merely a patriotic movement. They profess the freedom of religion and admit the spiritual ties between believers and their religious superiors, but by this same 'independence' I am today required to attack the representative of the Holy Father. Tomorrow I shall perhaps be forced to attack the representative of Jesus Christ, the Holy Father. The following day why should I not then be constrained to attack God Himself? . . .

"Since the Government has time and again insisted that they are not forcing us, but simply directing us, then I ought only to speak from my heart, and not have said 'yes' with my life, and 'no' in my heart. I ought only to sign those declarations to which I sincerely consent and not affix my name to those with which I disagree. If I live by deceit and fear death, I become a completely untrustworthy man, of use to no one. . . .

"I make these statements now being of a sane mind and I avow that whatever I may say later in a state of confusion will be entirely invalid. I am a Catholic and desire to love both my country and my religion. I do not wish discord between the two, but if the government cannot work harmoniously with religion, persecution will follow and many victims will be demanded from among Catholics. In such an event it is better that I die right now!"

The meeting broke up in confusion. On July 2, Father John Tung was arrested and has not been heard of since. Msgr. Riberi was expelled from China.

In January, 1951, the largest and longest-established mission, the China Inland Mission, gave orders for a complete evacuation of missionaries, 601 adults and 284 children. In an interview with *The Times* (February 19, 1951), the Secretary of the C.I.M., said:

"This will be the first mass withdrawal ordered since the Mission was established in 1865. Missionaries are not being illtreated, but they are made to feel that they are unnecessary.

"The Church in China was very strong, and at present enjoyed independence, but the ruling regime has made it clear that it will remain so only while it is free from outside influence. That meant that the missions were not getting the help they should from the churches."

The retreat from tolerance began with the United Nations' intervention in Korea in June, 1950. Newspapers throughout the country afterward published "Regulations for the Suppression of Counter-Revolutionary Activities," among which were listed: "Death penalty for bandits who are armed, for espionage rings and assassination gangs operating with counter-revolutionary objectives and *for the murder of public servants and people in general* [italics mine], the sabotage of factories, mines, warehouses, etc."

When China entered the Korean War in December, 1950, these regulations were intensified. The justification for the repressive policies was taken from the writings of Chairman Mao:

"You are not benevolent." Correct. We definitely have no benevolent policies towards the reactionaries or the counter-revolutionary activities of the reactionary classes. Our benevolent policy does not apply to such deeds or persons who are outside the ranks of the people; it applies only to the people."[20]

This was further developed in the *People's Daily* (Peking, *Jen Min Jih Pao,* December 13, 1950):

Cadres do not understand clearly and fully the Government policy. Some of our cadres have confused the severe suppression of counter-revolutionary activities with the consolidation of the united front, confused the objection to indiscriminate arrests and killings with the severe punishment of arch criminals, confused the suppression with magnanimity with the result that deviation of boundless magnanimity was not corrected in time.

The carrying out of the government policy meant that every suspected "counterrevolutionary" or "reactionary" had to write out an autobiography in full and complete detail from age seven to the present. Nothing was to be left out, including "the thoughts." To help the process along and make sure nothing was omitted, receptacles were posted in cities, towns, and villages into which people were asked to insert accusation slips, with information known to them about "suspicious elements."

Tens, then hundreds of thousands of people were arrested, imprisoned, and executed in huge public demonstrations and exhibitions. Not all of this persecution was against Christian "reactionaries." The "New Marriage Laws" of 1951, the desperate need for foreign exchange which produced a campaign of blackmail against overseas Chinese with relatives in China, the "three-anti" campaign (anti-bribery, anti-corruption and anti-bureaucracy) and others, all contributed their mounting thousands—millions—to the now nationwide terror.

A truck driver who escaped to Hong Kong gave the following account of his grisly task:

"I was conscripted by the Communists to drive one of their death trucks. I did not drive in the daytime, but at night. By far the greater number of executions were done secretly, and after dark. The victims were tied up hands and feet and loaded into our trucks like logs—120 of them to a truck. All night long I drove back and forth from the prisons to the river banks. The authorities didn't even bother with wasting shot on the victims. They were simply dumped into the river and drowned. I could not stand this nefarious traffic nor bear to hear the screams and moans of the helpless prisoners—so one day I jumped from the truck and fled."[21]

Miss Willis adds her sober record of the happenings at this time:

It was a terrible time [the summer of 1951]. The victim, nicknamed the "Tiger," would be placed at a table round which all his fellow workers were seated. All would point at him and shout Confess. No definite charges were made, but he would be told, We know you have committed a crime, confess, and you will be pardoned. This would go on and on until he confessed everything his accusers knew, and probably much more. . . . It was a wonderful opportunity for anyone who had a grudge, and many false accusations were brought. The tension in the city was terrible; business was paralyzed for months; many businesses failed. There were endless suicides; the favorite way was to jump off a high building, till people were almost afraid to walk along the streets. I think it was forty suicides a day were taken to one hospital alone, and there are dozens of hospitals in Shanghai; and many more were taken straight to the morgue. Finally, the Government had to stop the inquiries. The idea was good, and much corruption was cleared up, but the methods were terrible.[22]

By the end of 1952 what had existed of Christian missionary commitment for 140 years either had been completely eliminated or had taken on an entirely different character from that envisaged by those who had created or maintained the institutions. All the universities that had been founded and maintained on foreign Christian initiative had either been forcibly merged or had disappeared. *The Times,* (London) of September 27, 1952, reported these mergers and changes and concluded: "Thus ends the phase of missionary higher education in China which has lasted more than half a century; ironically, though perhaps inevitably, it has been ended by a regime in whose ranks many—perhaps even the majority—of its products are to be found."

A bitter note, indeed. Certainly, as the outside world watched the monumental and awesome drama being enacted in China, that part of the world concerned with the sphere of religion in the life of man, particularly Christianity, wondered what was likely to emerge from the fanatically revolutionary policies of these New Men in the New China. Would they, as they boasted, preside over the dissolution of all religion—including Christianity?

CHAPTER FOUR

The Communist Government and the Christian Organization

IN THE RAPID nineteenth- and early twentieth-century missionary expansion, China drew a majority of the finest representatives of Western Christianity. Notable converts in Britain, such as C. T. Studd and the famous "Cambridge Seven," in their new-found consecration thought first of China—and the same was true of America.

In no other period did the young people fling themselves recklessly into the Christian crusade as after 1890. Three of the student leaders at Yale, Horace Pitkin, Sherwood Eddy and Henry Luce went to Union Theological Seminary to prepare for the China mission field. Eddy later recalled: "When I would box every afternoon with Pitkin and when we would run our daily mile in the gym or the open air, we would say, 'This will carry us another mile in China.'" John R. Mott, organizer of the Student Volunteers at Cornell, declared that his field would be "the world" but China was the focal point. Eddy noted: "China was the goal, the lodestar, the great magnet that drew us all in those days."[1]

This was true not only of Christians in America and Britain, but in France, Germany, Italy, and other countries. China exerted a strange fascination on many different kinds of people from many countries—a fascination which exists to the present day. There are thousands of missionaries in Hong Kong and other parts of Asia who still look with longing toward the closed mainland of China. They anticipate as keenly as the Nationalists on Taiwan "the return to the mainland" to carry on their Christian activities, with the same zeal, if with a different emphasis, as before.

Protestant missionaries in China after World War I were divided into three distinct categories: the conservatives, the fundamentalists, and the liberals. Conservatives and fundamentalists agreed that the missionary's job was to lead individuals to conversion and salvation. The conservatives did not agree with the liberals but did not spend time and energy fighting them, while the fundamentalists did.

In 1920 the China Bible Union was organized by fundamentalist missionaries from every denomination in order to defend the doctrines held by the "great body of Evangelicals."[2] By 1921 the China Bible Union had 1,700 members among the missionaries, and by 1923 there were 2,000. The Union campaigned in the various denominations to have the financial support of liberals cut off, and to have their mission boards accept as future missionaries only those who subscribed to the statement of faith.[3]

There was also controversy over the China Sunday School Union, which was doctrinally conservative and published a great deal of the literature used by missionaries in their work. The liberals wanted to block the influence of the fundamentalists, and asked the World Sunday School Union to do something about it (the China Sunday School Union was largely supported by the WSSU). There was, naturally, opposition to this move, especially from the China Inland Mission. Eventually, however, the World Sunday School Union did withdraw its financial support.[4]

The bitterest attacks on both sides were carried on by only a few diehards. Charles Clayton Morrison, editor of the *Christian Century,* published an editorial in the March 12, 1930, issue, insisting that the only way Christians could be saved was for Christianity to identify itself with revolutionary social forces. He considered the fundamentalists the main obstacle in bringing about this identification.[5]

Both the conservatives and fundamentalists were basically non-political, and paid little attention to the economic problems of the farmers or industrial workers. They could describe the poverty and help alleviate it with food or financial relief, but the causes were vaguely understood to be that "too much land was given to growing opium" or "money was wasted on gambling."[6]

The liberals, on the other hand, took little interest in theology. Humanitarianism was the heart of the Christian gospel. They were impressed by the teachings of Confucius, by the long history and culture of China, by the desperate conditions of the peasants and the low state into which the country had fallen. They took less interest in "converting the heathen" than in emphasizing the social aspects of Christian teaching and of "Christianizing" Chinese society. Broadly speaking, therefore, the liberals concentrated on institutional work, while the conservatives and fundamentalists, with some exceptions, concentrated on evangelization work. The liberals tended to concentrate on cities, as centers of influence, while the others were found mostly in towns and villages—again, with certain exceptions.

As a result there were isolated pockets of Christian witness in both cities and rural areas, little islands of Western culture and Western denominational practice in the surrounding sea of China. This was a cause of considerable concern to Christian leaders as the 1940's drew to a close. There was also concern because the rural churches were not alive and growing and had never become an integral and vital part of the peasants' lives. In a letter from Peking in 1947, John Reisner commented on a statement by a noted Protestant missionary in China, Frank Price, that the very most that could be hoped for after another ten years was "1000 self-supporting, vital, growing rural churches." Reisner said: "After over 100 years of evangelistic effort—a great deal of it concentrated in rural China—is that all we have to show for it? In what lasting direction has all our expenditure of lives and funds gone? Why is there so little permanent rootage?"[7]

In contrast to the poor state of rural Christianity, there were more than one hundred thousand student applicants for ten thousand openings in the Christian universities and colleges which had more than seventy thousand students. But the country churches had little contact with the university world. Their pastors had little intellectual content in their preaching. And all too often missionary and Chinese pastor both bypassed the problems of rural life—landlordism, tenancy, usurious rates on loans.

At the same time, the Christian colleges and universities were not producing dynamic Christians either. They tended rather to be stepping stones to personal success in business or some profession. Perhaps 20 percent of the students showed some interest in campus religious life, but even these tended to stay in the cities after graduating and enjoy Western-style comforts. They were not really interested in the problems of rural life. In effect, then, the Chinese church produced no one (or very few) concerned to crusade for better society.[8]

Political and economic conditions under the Kuomintang government grew worse and worse. Olin Stockwell, a Methodist missionary in China who was later imprisoned by the Communists, says that the Kuomintang paid no attention to the social and economic problems that Communists focused on, called for loyalty to the government, but overlooked the terrible graft and corruption that sent prices and the cost of living soaring to new heights each month. And by this time it was so late nothing could be done.[9]

As a result, the Chinese people came to feel that any change would probably be for the better—even a Communist victory. Missionaries tended to side with the Kuomintang, in spite of the corruption, especially those who knew something of Communist methods. There were a few, however, who excitedly awaited the Communists— mostly younger missionaries with a social gospel—and who confessed to be "pink." Older missionaries tended to consider them naïve.[10]

When the Communists did actually take over the government of China in 1949, little action was taken against either Catholics or Protestants immediately. Official government policy was freedom of religion, not oppression. There were straws in the winds, however, of what their ensuing policy would be.

That summer an advisory commission consisting of five Protestants and two Buddhists was appointed for religious matters. Dr. Y. T. Wu, secretary of the Y.M.C.A., was one of the Protestants who agreed to serve on the Commission. His reactions are most interesting. Since religion according to Communist theory, he said, is part of any unhealthy social system, it would eventually disappear anyway. And "since Communism is practicing what Christianity merely professes, Christians have no right to stress the points on which they differ from the Communists, until they are similarly practicing their beliefs."[11]

Y. T. Wu (Wu Yao-tsung) has been perhaps the key leader of the Chinese church under communism. He was born into a non-Christian family in Canton in 1893, and became a Christian while he was studying at Customs College in Peking. He studied at two different times at Union Theological Seminary in New York after being ordained as a Congregational minister in 1920. In the 1930's he became the national literature secretary of the Association Press and was responsible for the publishing of several important religious books.

During the war with Japan, and during and after World War II, he became more and more interested in Communist theory. In 1948 he wrote an article for *Tien Feng* entitled "The Present-Day Tragedy of Christianity"[12] which castigated Protestantism for its association with capitalism, saying both were completely outmoded and unable to meet the needs of the time. Although he did not mention communism by name, the article talked favorably of the coming revolution, and by implication called for the Church to leave conservative reactionism behind. This article cost Wu the editorship of *Tien Feng,* but of course not for long.

In 1949 Wu attended the Communist-sponsored peace conferences in Prague and Paris. When he returned to China he wrote more articles influencing the Chinese church to accept the Communist regime, and soon he became the leader of the government program enforcing acceptance.

Most of the other Y.M.C.A. leaders followed Wu's example—Y. C. Tu, Kiang Wen-han, Liu Liang-mo, and Cora Deng, who was the national secretary of the Y.W.C.A. T. C. Chao, who was a president of the World Council of Churches and dean of the School of Religion at Yenching University, also welcomed the Communists. So did Bishop Z. T. Kaung, Senior Bishop of the Methodist Church. Robin Chen (Ch'en Chien-chen) Presiding Bishop of the Anglican Church (the Sheng Kung Hui) reluctantly came around to support the Communists. Another leader was H. H. Tsui, an Anglican layman and general secretary of the Church of Christ in China.

One Christian leader who was an ardent supporter of the Communist regime from the beginning—to the surprise and consternation of his friends in the West—was Marcus Cheng. He was an outstanding conservative leader, the president of Chungking Theological Seminary, an evangelical school. Marcus Cheng's autobiographical confession was published in *Tien Feng* for January 19, 1952.[13] In it he said:

> I finally awakened. Only the doctrine of Marx and Lenin give the science of revolution and the instrument which will set society free. . . . From the heart I can sincerely say that I fervently love Communism and accept the teaching of the Communist Party and the teaching of Mao Tse-tung . . . even as I accept astronomy and the fact that the earth is round or the statements in the Bible that the sun rises in the east and sets in the west. . . . There are some Christians who when they hear of my change of thinking and that I have joined the Communist Party and further that I have joined the Soviet-Russian Fellowship, think it very strange. Others freely abuse me. . . . Going through the studies and seeing the facts has caused me to hate America more than ever and through the same power to be drawn closer to the pure, loving friendship of Russia.[14]

Most of these leaders took part in the formation of the Three-Self Movement in 1949-50, which was described in Chapter Three, and which started with the issuing of the "Christian Manifesto." During these days there was still freedom to preach—but the preaching could not oppose communism.

A young Christian who attended a Communist political school in 1949 was told that "Jesus had failed because he had not understood the laws of social development. He had 'tried to leap directly from a slave society to the Kingdom of God.' 'Naturally this revolution was dialectically unsound and so did not work.'" In answer to the question "Can a Christian believe in the New Democracy?" the answer was yes: "Yes . . . but he cannot be an official worker in the party or the government."[15]

During these early days, missionaries began to sense that Chinese Christians and churches would rather not have them around and really considered them something of an embarrassment.[16] Many of them, who had not already done so, turned over their work to Chinese Christians and began the process of trying to leave China.

This was true for Roman Catholics as well. However, Bishop Walsh, of the Maryknoll Fathers, wrote to his colleagues in 1950, opposing their leaving voluntarily.

Nobody has any illusions about the Red determination to eliminate all religion. However, the question is: do we give them the field without the least struggle or do we keep at our work until we are put out? . . .

At a time when the Catholic religion is being traduced and persecuted with the design of eliminating it from China I think it is the plain duty of all Catholic missionaries—priests, Brothers, and Sisters, regardless of age, occupation and condition—to remain where they are until prevented from doing so by physical force. If internment should intervene in the case of some or even death, I think it should simply be regarded as a normal risk that is inherent in our state of life, as a necessary concomitant to our responsibilities and as a small price to pay for carrying out our duty. . . . In our particular case, moreover, I think that such an eventuality would be a privilege, too, because it would associate us a little more intimately in the Cross of Christ. . . .

Our vocation is not simply our vocational work—the teaching, preaching and village visiting we usually do. It is something much deeper, permanent, indelible. It does not change if our work is impeded, if we are in prison, or for any other reason. One of the necessary conditions to carry it out properly, I think, is to accept in advance every trouble and contingence in connection with it that Divine Providence puts in our way. If we start to pick and choose for ourselves, it is very hard to tell if we are carrying out our vocation or running away from it.[17]

Bishop Walsh obeyed his own directives, and refused to leave China when the Communists suggested it would be wise for him to do so. When he was put under house arrest, and the news reached papers outside of China, he became a symbol of the war between Christianity and communism.[18] Bishop Walsh's fate is discussed further in Chapter Eight.

The time of relative freedom for the Church came to an end in Aprill, 1951. That was when the government's denunciation movement began in Peking. The Religious Affairs Bureau of the government brought to Peking 151 Protestant leaders from all over the country for what was officially called a "Conference on Dealing with Christian Institutions Formerly Receiving American Aid." This was the birth of the Three-Self Reform Movement. The first organization was entitled the "Preparatory Committee of the China Christian (Resist American Help Korea) Three-Self Reform Movement Committee." It was set up under the presidency of the chairman of the Cultural, Educational and Religious Bureaus of the Government Administrative Council—Lu Ting-yi. In his inaugural address Lu stated: "The mission of the conference is to cut off thoroughly all relations between the Christian Church and American imperialism and to help the patriotic Christian to promote a new movement for independence, self-support, and independent propagation of the Faith, *so as to realize the decision of the Government Administrative Council.*"[19]

The Preparatory Committee consisted of twenty-five elected members. Its task was to direct the church in line with the Manifesto, that is on the basis of the "Three Selfs"—self-governing, self-supporting and self-propagating. This had been the express goal of missions in China since the early part of the century—but had never been completely realized, and funds had continued to pour into institutional work especially, until the Communist take-over.[20] The Communists gave the "Three Selfs" a slightly different twist—freedom from any kind of "imperialist" taint or relationship. This, of course, explained the "Reform" part of the Committee's title.

In his report on the first day of the Conference Y. T. Wu declared:

Most Chinese Christians love their country and are determined to cut off relations with imperialism and establish a church governed, supported and propagated by the Chinese people themselves. They enthusiastically support the Three-Self Reform Movement. Although imperialist elements hidden within the church have used every device to oppose and throttle the Three-Self Movement, even establishing a false Three-Self Movement to dissipate the strength of the Reform Movement, the Three-Self Reform Movement has still been able to grow and enlarge itself day by day. The number of Christians who have signed the Manifesto now exceeds 180,000. The imperialist plots have all been smashed by the strength of Christian patriotism.[21]

In order to reform the church and to expose every imperialist and antirevolutionary element, Christians were required to denounce publicly other Christians—missionaries and Chinese—who were considered reactionary or had any connection with imperialism. Southern Presbyterian Frank Price and Canton Y.M.C.A. secretary Edward Lockwood were two of the missionaries denounced. Some of the Chinese church leaders were Methodist Bishop W. Y. Chen, Anglican Bishop Y. Y. Tsü, Y.M.C.A. secretary S. C. Leung, and evangelist Ku Jen-en. The speeches had to be made by the closest friends and associates of the victims. Francis P. Jones rightly terms this method "diabolical," and adds, "The purpose . . . was to make the break with the former order of things as complete as possible, on the sound psychological theory that once you have denounced a former friend publicly your mind will automatically go on looking for further evidence to justify this betrayal of friendship."[22]

Within a week of the inaugural conference there were sixteen thousand arrests in Shanghai alone, and an unknown number committed suicide under the extreme pressures.[23]

At a huge "accusation meeting" organized by the Three-Self Reform Movement in Shanghai on June 10, 1950, representatives of all churches and Christian organizations were ordered to attend. It was also a requirement that they take part in the elaborate "rehearsals" beforehand. The rehearsals covered not only the speeches but the applause and the "spontaneous" reactions of the audience!

There were ten accusers from the larger religious groups so that their participation would have nationwide significance. All had had official "help" with their half-hour speeches in addition to all the rehearsals. Not even failure to produce an approved speech let one out of the situation. For instance, Miss Mary Liu of the Christian Literature Society had refused to accuse her missionary colleagues. Her preliminary speech was rejected for use in the accusation meeting, but what accusations it contained were written into a speech read by Y. T. Wu of the Society. Later, Mary Liu had to rewrite her speech complete with full accusations, and read it herself. And even that was not enough. When it was published in the newspapers, further denunciatory statements were added.[24]

The Reverend Leslie Lyall gives an account of the first huge meeting:

The eyes of Shanghai and also of the nation were on this first large-scale accusation meeting for the churches. The day dawned; it was as hot and humid as Shanghai can be in June. Each organization sent its participants in a group with its own leader, and everyone had a name card pinned to his clothes. The groups were instructed where to stand outside the stadium, where and when to enter. The groups assembled at half-past eleven. An hour and a half later they entered the stadium. It was blazing hot and a four-hour meeting lay ahead of them. Churchgoers were given seats in the covered stand, but mere employees of Christian organizations had to stand in the open on the scorching concrete. First-aid squads were kept busy helping those who fainted, while the speeches went on and on with their fantastic statements against the missionaries, made with faces contorted in feigned hate and calculated indignation. At six o'clock in the evening the crowd dispersed.

The next morning the daily papers carried lengthy accounts of the proceedings which had obviously been designed to inflict a severe loss of face on America, the missionary movement, and the Christian church itself.[25]

The Three-Self Movement accusation meetings were well organized (see Appendix III, "How to Hold a Successful Accusation Meeting") and skillfully coordinated at both national and local level. After being purged through self-criticism and accusation, a church or denomination could apply to the Three-Self Movement for permission to set up a "Reform church." The religious press supported the campaign with enthusiasm, each meeting being reported in detail and each victim having his crimes listed, with praise for the government for pursuing such actions. The campaigns were even justified on the basis of scripture in the religious journal *Tien Feng* ("Heavenly Wind") by quoting the precedent of Jesus as the first accuser in denouncing the Pharisees.[26]

While the Christians were "putting their house in order" (to use Chou En-lai's phrase) in line with the conference directive to "assist the Government to discover and punish antirevolutionary and corrupt elements within the Protestant church,"[27] the rest of the Chinese people were not forgotten. Everyone had to be indoctrinated with Communist ideals—the least peasant could not be overlooked. The result was that every social and economic group attended classes in political affairs—from factory workers to university professors. An integral part of such classes were the confessional meetings in which every citizen had to undergo both self-criticism and group criticism.

Local Three-Self Reform Committees were responsible for the reeducation and indoctrination of ministers and church members. Classes were held every week as a rule, though some times meetings were held every day for a period of weeks. In Shanghai in 1952, 362 pastors and church leaders signed up for classes. At Changsha there were 16 study groups for Christians. Part of the study was economic. Nanking Christians studied for two weeks "how the church could conform to the government demand to increase production and decrease waste."[28]

For all Christians the main aim was to find and root out imperialist ideas left over from the missionary era. Everyone was "helped" by the others, particularly if they had difficulty ridding themselves of such poison. Further help, if necessary, came from public accusation meetings, not on such a grand scale as the original Shanghai production, but very similar. Neighbors and friends were expected to denounce any reluctant or recalcitrant Communist-on-the-make, and make public their political and imperialist crimes. The result was generally imprisonment, sometimes death.

When Madame Pandit, the sister of India's Prime Minister, Jawaharlal Nehru, visited China in 1952, a group of Chinese Catholics sent her a letter describing the conditions of both foreign and Chinese Christians in prison:

It is not part of our present intention to give details of the religious persecution which is at present raging in China. It is well known that, with the exception of a few large cities, the freedom of worship laid down in the Constitution is nothing but a mockery. . . . In this letter we want to draw special attention to the fate of the Christian prisoners who were herded into the jails in their hundreds, on the pretext of having committed crimes against their country, although their real crime lay in their religious convictions. They were arrested at any hour of the day or night, in the streets or in their homes, often without a formal charge. . . . The dungeons and cells of these prisons are so overcrowded that the unfortunate inmates cannot always stretch themselves out full length, and have to take it in turns to go to sleep. In these cells, which are like ice in winter and ovens in summer, the prisoners have to sit motionless on the ground from dawn to dusk. It is an offense even to shut their eyes, and anyone who falls asleep is awakened by an angry roar from the guard. For days or weeks or months the monotony of this regime is only broken by the interrogations.

At these sessions the prisoner has to face his malignant judges, seeking to trap him with every question, alone, without the help of a counsel. He has only his memory to help him recall what he has said on previous occasions, for he is not allowed to note down his replies or details of the questions, and if he has to make a written deposition, he may not take a copy of it.

If his responses are considered insufficient or insolent, or if he refuses to speak altogether, he is kept standing at attention for hours or days.

Chains and manacles are loaded on to his hands and feet causing them to swell up immediately; thus pinioned to the walls of his cell like a wild animal, he has to remain until he begs for mercy and consents to speak.

This is the truth about the prisons of China, which you were not allowed to see during your visit.[29]

This tremendous experiment in "brainwashing"—or "thought-reforming," to use a more modern term—a whole nation, or a considerable part of a nation, was carried out on a simplified Pavlovian system. The alternation of heat and cold, the alternated talking sessions with solitary confinement, the switching lights on and off to give a one-hour-long day or a thirty-six-hour-long night, the order against sleeping, are the accepted Pavlovian techniques to throw the mind off balance—and this was much more easily accomplished when a person was physically weakened.

If the person proved stubborn, his connections with his family, friends, and the normal outside world were severed, creating a feeling of uncertainty and isolation along with physical and mental fatigue. Then the "group therapy" stage was introduced, and the group would be allowed to discover that one of them was an informer. This would increase the tension. Finally would come the confession and autobiography in minute detail.

The whole process was designed to uncover a person's weaknesses, preferably to have the subject find his own for greater effect; hence the emphasis on "self-criticism" meetings. The result was to produce what is technically known as "abreaction"—a state of complete nervous collapse, dilated pupils, rigid body, skin perspiring, breathing quick and shallow, then hysterics and loss of control. During World War II the same condition was found in soldiers afflicted with "shell shock" or "battle fatigue." Later it was discovered that this condition could be created by drugs alone by injecting insulin into the bloodstream.

In his book *Battle for the Mind,* William Sargant has pointed out significant similarities between the symptoms of a climactic spiritual conversion and the "abreaction" techniques of "brainwashing."[30] And it was evident, whether by design or coincidence, that the new Communist government of China was following the same pattern in its techniques of "thought-reform." It was a new "messianic" vision which the Communist leaders preached to the people of China—the highly moral religious strain, the certainty of "correctness," the undeviating belief in certain dogmas, the assumption that virtue was inherent in the working class and their Communist representatives, the new doctrine of the elect, the future reward. All this had been uniquely revealed to Chairman Mao Tsetung and communicated to the people of China through his faithful disciples, who in turn urged their followers to make disciples "unto the uttermost parts of the earth."

Again there was a striking parallel with Christianity in the methods used to spread this new Communist "gospel." "Revival meetings" of all kinds were held all over China, to tell doubters and "sinners" to repent of their transgressions, confess their troubles, and see the light. Then they would be expected to follow the true way, just as new Christians are expected to live a new life. And like new Christians the new converts were helped, encouraged, and disciplined by their fellows.[31]

In addition to the hundreds of thousands of Chinese Christians who were subjected to the mass application of the above techniques, several foreign missionaries were selected for special treatment. Among these was Geoffrey Bull, who has given a detailed account of his three-year imprisonment and interrogation from 1950-53, in his book *When Iron Gates Yield*.

Those preliminary and nebulous questionings, I realized afterwards, are the "dialectical" approach to interrogation. It is necessary to find out the whole course of development of a person's life from earliest days. The dominant influences and conflicts. His social position and class background, the nature of his environment and social contacts and relationships at various stages of his growth. The type of education, his early political loyalties and the big crises of his life. Only after this ground is fairly clear can the attitude of the Government be determined in regard to interrogation and "brain-washing."[32]

. . . Full interrogation on an ever-increasing scale now began. George's movements and mine were investigated step by step, all causes and motives being ruthlessly ferreted out.

. . . With increased pressure everything came to a head one night. . . .

. . . The night of my decision I slept poorly, tossing back and forth on the hard boards. . . . I considered I had been fair to them in telling them the truth, but they now became adamant and I entered one of the most terrible periods of my life.

Day after day I endured constant interrogation. Sometimes four times a day I was hauled out before different officers and tribunals. A special senior officer interviewed me twice. Military and civil officials were called in. They had me standing, sitting, they used countless methods and conversational sessions. They covered the same ground over and over again. . . . Their torture became more vile.

. . . Day after day the threat of execution continued. . . .

My interrogations took a new turn. Night after night I was awakened up and interrogated into the early hours of the morning. . . . These night sessions were fearful. . . .[33]

. . . On the wall behind the officials were placed huge pictures of Chairman Mao Tse-tung and Chu De. . . . On either side were pasted slogans outlining the policy of the Government towards the prisoner. "Confess your crime and live! Hide it and you die! Suppression and leniency combined! Acknowledge your sin, reform your thoughts and strive for new life in the service of the people!"[34]

Through the use of these techniques on both foreign missionaries and Chinese Christians, the new Communist government had succeeded, by the end of 1951, in isolating the Protestant church in China from all relationship with the churches of the outside world. But there was still a powerful and vocal opposition to the new Communist regime's attempts to eliminate Christianity in the many national indigenous churches which were now emerging from their pre-1949 obscurity by the pressure of circumstances.

For instance, Wang Ming-tao, a lay preacher in Peking and one whose writings were extremely influential throughout the Protestant fundamentalist churches in China, was implacably opposed to both the Three-Self Reform Movement and the Communist government, and publicly said so. Writing toward the end of 1951 in his quarterly magazine, the *Spiritual Food Quarterly,* he said:

At that time [1927, when he first published the magazine] I already knew that if in this present time I faithfully proclaimed the Word of God—rebuking the sins, the evils and the doctrine-destroying teachings in the corrupted, nominal church—I should surely meet the opposition and persecution which met Martin Luther. But there was one slight difference. The Church today is not faced with as great an opponent as that power of the Roman Church in the sixteenth century. Therefore, it could not with authority and power crush one who faithfully preached the Word, though it would unwillingly see men rise up to point out the depths of corruption and doctrine-denial to which the Church had sunk. Under these conditions the one who faithfully preaches the Word of God cannot but expect to meet opposition from some leaders in the Church and from "Christians" who are spiritually dead, in the form of malicious slander and abuse. I know that this will come to pass. I am prepared to meet it. I covet the courage and faithfulness of Martin Luther.[35]

By the end of 1952 the Three-Self Reform Movement reported success in their objectives. Imperialistic influences were being cut away, there was loyalty of all Christians to the government and to the Oppose-America-Aid-Korea Movement, church leaders and lay members were united because of the purging experiences, and many churches had fulfilled the requirements of becoming full-fledged members of the Three-Self Reform Church.[36]

The first Chairman of the Movement, Y. T. Wu, in an article entitled "How the Communist Party Has Educated Me," described the typical attitude of New China's new Three-Self Reform Church Christians as they were at that period and as they were likely to be for some time to come:

It is due solely to the Chinese Communist Party that the Chinese people today can stand erect, receive these blessings and have such a bright outlook for the future. . . .

In the early period . . . I was anti-Communist. . . . But the cannon shots of September 18 (1931) awakened me. The development of the movement for saving the nation made me gradually drop my prejudices against the Communist Party. In Shanghai I joined the Save the Nation party, and I began to realize that Communist thinking and the Communist road of struggle were the only way to save China. . . .

. . . Today under the direction of the Communist party, all of China has been liberated, the Chinese Christian revolutionary movement is spreading throughout the country, and the thinking of many Christians has already undergone a fundamental change. Much that yesterday was impossible and wrong has become today possible and right. If the "miracles" that Christianity believes in are true, then the fact that the Chinese Communist Party in the short space of thirty years has enabled the Chinese people, exploited and oppressed for thousands of years, to stand upon their feet, and at the same time enabled the Christian Church to throw off the shackles of imperialism, is a miracle of a sort heretofore unheard of. . . .[37]

CHAPTER FIVE

Problems of an Indigenous Church in Communist China

ONE OF THE MOST OUTSTANDING features of the generation preceding 1949 was the development of "indigenous" Chinese churches.

We have seen that for some time before and during this period there was a gradual progression in the Christian churches, Protestant and Catholic, from a general policy of "paternalism" to one of "fraternalism." But at the most all this had accomplished was a measure of Sinification of the Western religious and denominational systems. They were not truly "indigenous" in the sense of "native," "belonging naturally," growing out of the spiritual soil of China.

Each system, Roman Catholic and Protestant, and each denomination and sect, faithfully reflected its Western origin and practice in ecclesiology, liturgy, and idiosyncracies, even where there were Chinese pastors or elders. Further, when Chinese evangelization organizations began to emerge, such as the "China Evangelistic Band," the "Christian Workers Mission," the "Back to Jerusalem Band," they tended to be modeled on similar Western organizations already in existence in China.

The truly indigenous churches which sprang to life in the early part of the twentieth century in China owed nothing to Western denominational influences, although in many instances the leaders had been personally influenced by spiritual individuals in the denominations and sects. But the groups themselves were spontaneous outgrowths of Christian witness derived from the Bible alone—sometimes after recourse to the original texts, not just the Chinese or English versions; and in consequence the distinctive forms in which they emerged were wholly Chinese in interpretation and practice.

When the Three-Self Reform Movement was initiated, with its emphasis on "self-government, self-support, and self-propagation," one unique result of the campaigns was to throw into prominence the existence and widespread acceptance of many Chinese churches which already conformed to the "three-self" principles through spiritual conviction, not by government order.

But with a considerable difference. The government's Three-Self Reform Movement was directed toward self-government from imperialist control, self-support from imperialist money, and self-propagation away from imperialist "poison." The indigenous churches were self-governing through strict conformity to New Testament principles of church gathering and discipline, self-supporting through New Testament principles of individual and corporate responsibility of voluntary contributions, and self-propagating through New Testament conviction of no necessity for clergy or ordination, and individual responsibility to communicate the gospel. It was inevitable that there must be a head-on clash with the new Communist government and with the government-controlled Three-Self Reform Movement. From the government's side it was going to be difficult to insist on a "reform" to "three selfs" among the indigenous groups where no obvious necessity existed. The very fact that the indigenous churches went so far beyond the government in their three-self New Testament principles was only one aspect of the problem. Such autonomy also meant that every church and every individual would have to be dealt with separately; and, more important, that each local church and each individual was without the "guilty associations" of foreign parent churches so necessary for intimidation. Finally, each of these Chinese Christians was as convinced a believer in Christ and His teachings as the new Chinese Communists were in Chairman Mao and his writings.

The earliest and most widespread of these churches was the "True Jesus Church." This was begun by Paul Wei in 1917, after he had sold all that he possessed and gone out to preach. The first True Jesus Church was in Tientsin; then the movement quickly spread to Peking and other provinces. The emphasis was on communal living and following the example of the early apostolic church. Later these churches sprang up outside China—in Taiwan, Korea, Japan, and Southeast Asia. The True Jesus Churches are fundamentalist, emphasizing faith healing and "tongues," but the early communal living feature of the founders has now been discontinued.[1]

In 1952 Isaac Wei, the son of the founder of the movement, under pressure from the Communists wrote out an article entitled "My Self-Examination" in which he gave an account of the movement and its practices.

The True Jesus Church was founded by my late father Paul Wei in Peking on May 1, 1917, and has now had a history of nearly 35 years. I have worked in it throughout the whole period. It has had a rapid growth. Its local churches, large and small, in China and abroad, now number about a thousand, with about 100,000 baptized spiritual brothers and sisters. . . .

I used to think that since our church has had no relations with American imperialism and has never been supported financially by reactionaries or bureaucrats, it would be hard to find anything in the Church to denounce. . . . But after the summer study institute in Peking (summer of 1951) the eyes of my heart have been enlightened so that I have now honestly and deeply realized that I myself have been pro-American and against Soviet Russia, the Party and the People. . . .

. . . I wish to admit frankly and without regard to face that the "Three-Self" church which I preached was not thoroughgoing, it was only an unconscious tool of imperialism, feudalism and bureaucratic capitalism. For example, my teaching of being above politics, above country, above the world and above class was just the result of imperialist poisonous thinking, yet I complacently thought that this was true spirituality. . . .

Our "self-support" idea was also inadequate. Although it is true that we did not use the financial support of imperialism and reactionary governments, still our country churches depended to a great extent on the financial support of feudalistic landlords, and to tell the truth I had never denounced feudalism. Also our preachers were all taken out of production, we had not followed Paul in laboring day and night to support ourselves, and so in many places our church after the land reform faded away, because our method of "self-support" had been to depend on the landlords. . . .

In "self-government" our record is still more shameful. Although we had denounced the greed and corruption of the old society, still our church welcomed the bureaucrats and capitalists of the cities. . . . We often elected bureaucrats and capitalists to responsible positions in the church . . . . anyone with money and influence, if he only showed a little piety, would be sure to be elected, and there were even some who did not truly love the Lord who got elected. . . .

The largest of the indigenous churches was, and is, the "Little Flock," a name given to them because of a quotation from the Gospel of John used in their hymnbooks. The name used by themselves is "Christian Assemblies"; but there is no association with the "Christian Assemblies" or "Plymouth Brethren Assemblies" of the West, although their principles of church gathering, discipline, and teaching emphasis are strikingly similar.

The "Christian Assemblies" movement began in 1926 through the teaching of a remarkable Chinese Christian, Nee To-sheng, more widely known as Watchman Nee. Nee was a man of brilliant mind, a research scientist, and deeply spiritual. He founded a large pharmaceutical factory and many chemist shops throughout China. Both the profits from these operations and the operations themselves were used to support evangelists and teachers, print booklets and books, and finance other aspects of Christian witness.

Watchman Nee had been influenced by a Western business colleague, a member of the Exclusive Brethren; and after a period of private study of the Bible, he began to expound the Scriptures with great clarity and power. He emphasized the autonomy of the local church, the fellowship of all Christian believers, whatever their denomination, the scripturally unwarrantable practice of denominationalism and its inadequacy, and the tremendous promise of a New Testament Christianity in China.

Many Chinese Christians began leaving their denominations for the simple household "Christian Assemblies," particularly in Fukien and Chekiang Provinces. When Watchman Nee's exposition of the Acts of the Apostles was published under the title *Concerning Our*

Missions, the stream became a flood, including many foreign missionaries. From among these early associates there emerged many evangelists and teachers of power and ability who carried the new emphasis across the country.

When I was first brought into touch with the movement in 1946, they had a huge meeting place, "Christian Assembly," in Shanghai, capable of holding three thousand believers, and there were hundreds of others throughout China. They kept no register of churches or members, but one report claimed that by 1949 there were more than seven hundred churches with a membership of over seventy thousand.[2]

With the collapse of the traditional denominations and organizations in 1950 and the subsequent pressures of the Three-Self Reform Movement on them, many of the regular members, having no churches to attend, joined the "Christian Assemblies," so that there was a spectacular rise in membership. Writing in 1961, Leslie Lyall claimed: "There are thousands of such assemblies throughout China, many of them having separated from older churches, but many also having been independent from their beginnings."[3] Another report— from a Communist source—stated that in the mid-1950's they were "more numerous than all the other Protestant denominations combined."

The most interesting and unusual of the indigenous churches was undoubtedly the "Jesus Family." It was started in Shantung by a converted Buddhist, Ching Tien-ying, mostly from among Methodist churches in the province. He and two women missionaries had thrown themselves enthusiastically into evangelical work with a strong emphasis on holiness of life and this had drawn the disfavor of the more orthodox among the Methodist community. Ching Tien-ying then sold all his possessions, gave the proceeds to the poor, and set up his first communal Christian society in the village of Ma-chuang, in Shantung, in 1921.

A few of his friends joined him, and the community began to organize itself into the pattern that was to be followed in the future. Farming was begun, a cooperative store opened, a silk-weaving industry started, and a chapel built. The basis for their community was the example of the early Christians, of whom it was said in *The Acts of the Apostles* that "they had all things common." The leader of each community, as they spread, first had to sell his land

and give it to the poor as a prerequisite of leadership, and afterward he was the "least" or most humble of the community.

A free translation of one of their hymns reads:

Love is the organizing principle of the House of Jesus. This is a heavenly conception, and man had small part in its growth. Since we are fathers and sons by grace and brothers in the Spirit, leadership is weak and bodily life is very strong. All are "one in Christ," whether old or young, male or female, dull or gifted. All worldly differences are ignored, tribe or nation, rich or poor, honorable or lowly. Truly our aim is, "Thy kingdom come, Thy will on earth be done."

The structure of the "Jesus Family" community was a pyramid, with agriculture as the base and the chapel as the apex. On the agricultural base were built the various departments, such as carpentry, shoemaking, bakery, smithy, machine shop and electrical department, stone masonry, schools and kindergarten, printing, bookbinding, financial and "outside relations" departments—everything to make the community self-sufficient.

The church was the apex, and all of the community's activities flowed to it and from it—literally. The chapels were used as workshops, where weaving, spinning, knitting and shoemaking were carried on, only ceasing when the services were about to begin. They were so much a part of the communities' life that later, when the Communist government came into power, the Communist propaganda meetings were held in the same place, alternating with the work and church services. Of course, many of the "chapels" were no more than large rooms in private houses.

The "Jesus Family" spread in the following way: A new convert in a village would adapt a room in his house for services for his neighbors. When others were converted the nucleus of a "community" would be set up; and because of the impact of their spiritual witness and manner of living, it was not long until the whole village or district became a "community."

Dr. Vaughan Rees, who lived with the Jesus Family from 1948 to 1950 has said that the situation was remarkably similar to that in England during Wesley's time when he was forced to exclaim: "How can I prevent those lately converted to Christ from becoming wealthy? The wasteful become frugal, diligence replaces sloth, and the loveless become loving. How can such people remain poor or indigent?"

Thus one of the problems of the "Jesus Family" communities was the accumulating wealth. Rather, it would have been had they not solved it by a system of "tithing," which meant that they gave away sometimes 10 percent, and sometimes as high as 90 percent, of their income to the surrounding poor. One community was reported to have given away everything, except the food they ate, and for the rest looked to God with simple faith to supply other needs.

Dr. Rees's little book on his experiences with the community in Ma-chuang includes the following observations:

That piece of land was [originally] about three acres but through additions has now grown to its present size of forty to fifty acres and supports about five hundred people. . . .

Foreign pigs and a modern pigsty, a big Hereford bull and milch cows immediately met my eyes as we entered through the wall of trees. In Chinese villages glass is a rare curiosity. Here it is used in all the fowl houses. Electricity in China is unknown except in the big towns. Here the rooms have electric light, and over the big central well is an electric pump. . . .

In Ma-Chuang their livestock consisted of horses, mules, one blind donkey, cattle, pigs, geese, fowls, ducks and rabbits. The kitchens were large and well arranged, and all the utensils were made and cast in the blacksmith's department, even the large steam pressure cooker. . . .

One day a typical group of them [Communists] came and called loudly for the pastor. . . . I saw him in the distance. He was pushing the manure cart, and he pushed it right into their midst before someone said "Here he is." The Communists had drawn back from the offensive cart. They then wanted to know how he could keep adequate discipline, when he did such a menial job.

Chow-shin-ming, the pastor and official head of the community, explained that since they were all equal, he the leader had the privilege of doing the worst jobs. The Communists looked sheepish. . . ."[4]

Ching Tien-ying was in general charge of the communities, as well as being head of the original Ma-chuang community. By 1941 there were 141 different communities in eight provinces, the larger number of them in Shantung, with approximately 6,000 members.[5] Like the other indigenous groups the "Jesus Family" expanded rapidly as conditions deteriorated in the late 1940's and at the beginning

of the 1950's when so many Chinese Christians were forced to leave
the traditional denominations, but no definite number is known.

Among the more recently established indigenous groups was the
Ling Liang (Spiritual Food) World-Wide Evangelistic Mission,
established in Shanghai in 1942 by the Rev. Timothy Dzao. During
the Sino-Japanese war Dzao built one church and a tabernacle in
Shanghai holding about two thousand people. Other churches were
begun in Southeast Asia; and since 1950 two large congregations,
supporting Chinese missionaries, have been started in Hong Kong.

In addition to the above groups, there were many other small
and unconnected groups scattered throughout the country, but they
were usually too small to be effective other than locally.

In a nation of some 600,000,000 in 1947 the total membership
of these indigenous groups was proportionately very small, but their
influence was out of all proportion to their numbers in the places
where they were represented. They were conspicuously *not* "rice
Christians," those who were Christians only for what they could get
out of it. They were very definitely *not* foreign missionary controlled
or supported, and those associated with the various groups were not
only convinced Christians but obviously enjoyed being so. There
was no race or class distinction, so often such a distinctive feature
of the traditional denominations and organizations; and peasants,
workers, doctors, professors, military, and officials shared spiritual
and pastoral responsibilities.

All of these factors, and several more, were sources of strength
to the groups when the mounting Communist pressures were put on
Chinese Christians after 1950. Religion in China, especially Christianity, had fitted into such a standard pattern that the formulas and
slogans of communism borrowed from Europe and Soviet Russia
seemed to be tailor-made to fit the situation. When there was little
or no conformity to that pattern, the new Chinese Communist
regime found it extremely difficult to handle a situation for which
there were no Communist textbook answers.

The situation, and the critical problem it contained for the Communist and Christian, was admirably described by the Anglican
missionary, David M. Paton:

. . . we are faced with the débris of one dead doctrine, and the competition of two extremely alive ones. The dead doctrine of progress sustained our fathers in the carrying of capitalist democratic culture to most parts of the globe. Its core was the conviction that in thus extending the range of western liberal culture and developing its assumptions, they were in effect establishing on earth that which would grow into the kingdom of God. . . . That whole view exists today only as débris, for it has foundered on the rocks not so much of human sin, as of the contradictions and complexities of the very western culture which was the substance of its belief.

It is otherwise with Marxism. From our point of view, Marxism is the older doctrine of progress brought up to date by absorbing—indeed giving pride of place to—the contradictions of capitalist society which caused the liberal failure of nerve. The Marxist at all events believes that in history there is a movement, dialectical, stormy, checked here and there, but finally and certainly advancing, to the goal of the classless society which may be postponed but cannot fail of achievement, and in which all human strivings and yearnings will be fulfilled; and of this movement he is the servant. Whatever his personal distresses and failures, he is justified, for he is on the side of history and humanity. He understands the drift of history, and sets himself scientifically to advance it. The day may not dawn in his time, but that it will dawn he knows, and he knows also that its dawning is hastened by his labours.

On the other side of conventional Christianity are the adventist sects. They also see in the events of our time a revolutionary situation, and set themselves to take advantage of it. But it is a revolution of another sort altogether; it is the End of which the New Testament speaks, and the wars and civil wars, the famines, riots and disturbances are the signs of the End, the harbingers of Armageddon, as the explosions of atomic energy are the fulfilment of II Pet. 3:10. These men also have hope in history; and their preaching takes on a renewed and practical urgency as they seek by their witness to discover the elect and to save them from the wrath to come.[6]

The establishment of the Communist government in Peking in 1949 crystallized the dilemma of many Chinese Christians. In the dedication of their Communist fellow countrymen to dialectical materialism they saw the superficiality of the humanist "social gospel" to which they had been asked to give their allegiance. They were quick to reject the superficial and inadequate, not out of apostasy or disloyalty to former missionary friends and colleagues, but because the hypothesis was wrong and the choice put to them false. Now they had a clear choice: to accept the Marxist interpretation of history and society and reject the Western-imported liberal version of Christianity; or to accept the "adventist," or fundamentalist, indigenous New Testament and Christ-centered version of history and society and reject the imported Marxist interpretation as superficial and inadequate.

In a revolutionary setting the issues were no longer obscure, and St. Augustine's analysis was seen to be relevant: "The kingdoms of this world are founded on *superbia,* man's claim to be his own master and his own god; the kingdom of Christ is founded on *humilitas,* the submission of man to a power outside himself that both judges and saves."

To quote David Paton again:

The result [of professional clericalism exported to the mission field] at all events is evident: it is sterility. Immense energies are occupied, as they are in England, by simply keeping things going; if the ecclesiastical organisation in England is out of date and irrelevant, how much more so in China. . . .

A sacramental system that is exalted but practically unusable falls into contempt. The indigenous sects already referred to spread their influence. If your own Church cannot provide you with an effective ministry and frequent sacraments, and is not organised, whatever its formal theology, in such a way that you feel you are a member of a spiritual fellowship, you will (if you mean business) more often than not join some other which can provide these blessings, whatever its other failings. One of the most widely spread of these sects has, in the manner of the Plymouth Brethren, a breaking of bread for believers each Sunday and is both a real and expanding fellowship."[7]

The indigenous groups placed varying emphasis on different aspects of Christian doctrine but, generally speaking, there was little difference. They would meet several times a week for prayers, teaching, Bible study, "breaking of bread" or communion, and fellowship. At these gatherings either a pastor—unordained, chosen from among themselves—or more often one of the male members gifted with preaching or teaching ability would be responsible for expounding the Scriptures. The Christians would meet in simply designed halls, in private houses, or in rented buildings; the congregations would vary from thirty or a hundred to a thousand or three thousand. The money for the buildings, or the many activities, was obtained from the members either by tithing—giving a percentage of one's income, usually a minimum of ten percent—or by voluntary contributions.

Among the influential "Christian Assemblies," the leaders were never selected or appointed—they "emerged." That is, in the words of the New Testament, a bishop "must be blameless, the husband of one wife, vigilant, sober, of good behaviour, given to hospitality, apt to teach; not given to wine, no striker, not greedy of filthy lucre; but patient, not a brawler, not covetous" (I Timothy 3:1-13). They maintained that the New Testament churches were ruled by elders (*presbyteroi*) and deacons, and that the elders could equally well be called overseers or bishops (*episkopoi*). Some made a distinction between bishops and elders, but it was generally agreed that this was a distinction of function and not of status; i.e., all bishops were elders, though not all elders functioned as bishops. These groups conformed to the New Testament, too, in that there was no *single* elder or bishop in a church, but always several.

The function of the bishops or elders might be classed as administrative, in that they were the authorized "shepherds of the flock" and were responsible for the spiritual conduct of the members of their church and the church's activities. In addition there were men recognized as "evangelists" and "teachers." The former were responsible for preaching to the non-Christians and making converts, and the latter for the building up of the Christian person or community. All of these men were recognized because of the particular spiritual qualities which they manifested; hence, they were seen to "emerge" and were never "appointed" as elders, evangelists, or teachers. When the spiritual quality disappeared through complacency, sin, or any other reason, their authority was also automatically suspended.

Each local church was completely autonomous. In addition to the local church in any village, town or city, there were many "household churches." (Very often there were more than one "meeting hall" in any large town or city. The "local church" would be the accepted meeting place in the particular district, and they would be known as "Hall Number One," "Hall Number Two," and so on. Each was autonomous, but the aggregate was known as the "local church" of the town or city.) There would be gatherings held in private houses for neighbors "to hear the gospel of Christ," or for a few friends meeting for prayer or Bible discussion, or for classes for children or young people. But these were not recognized as "churches" in the

New Testament sense; they were only complementary activities carried on by members on their own initiative. The chief aim was always the upbuilding of the local church.

The foregoing description of the variegated activities of the indigenous churches, with their deeply held convictions, shows that the new Communist regime was faced with a considerable problem, or variety of problems. Also, a Communist regime could not tolerate such communities or practices, for they struck at the very roots of many of communism's most cherished ideals.

This was particularly true of the "Jesus Family" communities, where Communist ideals were being carried out in Christ's name and in a spirit of love, instead of in Marx's name and by official decree.

On one occasion when some Communists were being escorted through a Jesus Family community, one of them asked a Jesus Family leader, "How do you prevent your people from stealing the grapes?" They had just made stealing on the communal farms "a sin against the people and punishable by death"; yet stealing still went on occasionally. The simple answer was: "If anyone has the Lord Jesus in his heart, he does not steal."[8] What the Communist made of that is not recorded.

The Jesus Family communities had "fly-killing" campaigns with prizes for the greatest number killed, long before the Communist government popularized the campaigns and made "people's heroes" out of their champions.[9] It would be interesting to know just how much the Communists were influenced by these Jesus Family communities, for they were most influential in Shantung and were often under different political regimes in the civil struggle before 1949.

While the manner of life of the Chinese Christians of the indigenous churches was irreproachable, even surpassing the Communists in their recognition of social responsibilities and love for their neighbors, the Communists could not ignore the very anti-Communist beliefs. Even if they had wanted to, they could not, for the Christian leaders of these groups were often vociferous in their denunciation of the traditional denominations, the Three-Self Reform Movement, and the government itself.

Wang Ming-tao, the pastor of an independent fundamentalist church in Peking, a powerful preacher whose writings were widely read and respected by Christians throughout China, was an implacable opponent of liberal theology in general and the Three-Self

Reform Movement in particular. In turn he represented all that they opposed. He and Watchman Nee stood in the way of the government's attaining its declared goal of a "united church" under government control. Not only did he denounce the liberal theology and the Three-Self Movement in general terms, but he would uncompromisingly take up statements made by individuals and, naming them in public, would denounce them as traitors and deceivers. Since these men were exactly the type of Christians which the new regime wanted, they became the leaders of the Three-Self Reform Movement and spearheaded the attacks on Wang Ming-tao and all fundamentalist indigenous churches.

But thousands continued to crowd into Wang Ming-tao's church. And he continued to attack the Three-Self Movement. The church was separate and holy in the world. It could not "come to terms with the world without compromise, he declared. By implication, a church which was entangled in the affairs of this world, its politics and policies, a church which had become the meek servant of an atheist government, had ceased to function as the true church of Jesus Christ."[10]

In 1952 the Communists and the Three-Self Reform Movement increased their pressures; but Wang Ming-tao was still either too prominent or too powerful, or the government was not yet ready with their case against him, for the government to take action. But in April, 1952, during the "Five-Anti" campaign, Watchman Nee of the "Little Flock" was arrested on five charges of being a capitalist, found guilty of all five crimes, and sentenced without trial to fifteen years' imprisonment.

In February, 1953, *Tien Feng* published the condemnation of Ching Tien-ying, founder and head of the "Jesus Family." He had been denounced by a nephew who accused him of "avarice, tyranny and sexual irregularities." The Shantung Jesus Family was dissolved, followed by the dissolution of the Nanking communities.

Throughout the country there was launched a determined effort to bring everyone under the direct control of the government. In the sphere of Christianity this meant that all churches, traditional and indigenous, must be subordinate to the Three-Self Reform Movement.

CHAPTER SIX

The Communist Solution for a Protestant Church

THE YEAR 1953 OPENED for the Communist leaders in Peking with considerable optimism. In 1949 Mao Tse-tung had promised the Chinese people that the new Communist government would eliminate the landlord, bureaucratic and capitalist classes, reject the West, and "lean to one side" in allying China with the Soviet Union. By 1953 two phases of their program had been efficiently if ruthlessly executed, and the third was well on its way to realization in political and economic spheres.

Inside China the most rigid form of government the Chinese people had ever experienced insured absolute obedience to its decrees. Rice production was rising. Taxes were collected. Trains ran on time. Millions of people were bitterly unhappy, but it was not the sort of unhappiness that encouraged thoughts of rebellion against the regime. That possibility had been sufficiently scotched by the government's use of violence and fear in imposing dictatorship upon a people whose traditions were foreign to communism. The deliberate use of violence and fear as a matter of policy was no secret carefully hushed up by Peking. As a leading Hong Kong newspaper report told it:

Peking intended violence to breed fear and through newspapers and radio told the whole story. Millions of Chinese arrested as "counter-revolutionaries" were dragged before the "people's courts" and by public acclaim sentenced to death. All over the country these unfortunates died publicly in the streets of towns and villages, while frenzied mobs danced the Communist harvest dance and shouted for blood. Millions of others who atoned by public confession went to forced labour for life or were given sentences of death suspended for two years and the chance to "reform" under forced labour. . . . Observers in Hong Kong, at China's key-hole, seek patiently for any hint of the collapse they feel must come. But today there is no hint of any such development.[1]

The same unadorned list of facts showed that religious persecution was being waged on an equal scale. Occasionally statements were made that, no matter what happened in religious matters, the general material condition of the people was being improved.

Again, the reasons for taking these actions were not hidden away, but were publicly stated for all to read and understand. The present President of the Chinese People's Republic, Liu Shao-chi, wrote in 1950:

With us, therefore, everything is dependent on and determined by the people's consciousness and self-activity, without which we can accomplish nothing and all our efforts will be in vain. But as long as we rely upon the consciousness and self-activity of the masses and as long as such consciousness and self-activity are genuine, then with the additions of the Party's correct leadership, every aspect of the great cause of the Party will finally triumph. Therefore, when the masses are not fully conscious, the duties of Communists—the vanguard of the masses of the people—in carrying out any kind of work *is to develop their consciousness by every effective and suitable means* [italics mine]. This is the first step in our work which must be done no matter how difficult it is or how much time it will take.

Only when the first step has been taken can we enter upon the next step. In other words, when the masses have reached the necessary level of consciousness, it is then our responsibility to guide them in their actions—to guide them to organize and fight. When this is brought about, we may further develop their consciousness through their actions. This is how we lead the masses step by step to fight for the basic slogans of the people—put forth by the Party.[2]

Divested of jargon, what this meant in practice was that every individual in China would have to be made, by persuasion or force, to recognize the importance of the Communist Party line on every subject; and when its importance had been grasped, he was responsible for persuading others. In relation to Christianity, this policy meant that those Christians who had mastered the Communist Party's principles and purposes were now responsible to "guide others in their actions—to guide them to organize and fight." Hence the emphasis on the "consciousness and self-activity" of the Three-Self Reform Movement—to guide other Protestant Christians to accept the Party line, instead of just setting up a separate organization. This policy also explains why the authorities were so insistent that the Three-Self Reform Movement officials should persuade all other Christians to accept its authority.

It has been noted elsewhere (in Chapter One) how successful the Three-Self officials had been by 1953 in bringing Chinese Christians within their government-controlled representation. An important insight on how this was brought about has been provided by a Christian layman who lived under the Communist regime for ten years and who was a lay delegate to the Three-Self Movement during his time in China. In an article[3] describing his experiences throughout this period he said that his purpose was not to describe the formation of the Three-Self Reform Movement in 1951 "but the way these charges affected the churches in the city of Peking itself."

The Three-Self Reform Movement of Peking churches began in July, 1951, when the Religious Affairs Bureau of the Peking Municipal Government and the United Front Work Department of the Peking Committee of the Chinese Communist Party jointly sponsored "Learning Meetings" for all Christian churches of Peking Municipality. About three hundred ministers and church members attended the meetings which were held every morning for a month. Each day began with a brief prayer meeting, followed by a general assembly, during which reports would be made by leaders from the Religious Affairs Bureau and the United Front Department. The reports consisted of (1) current events, particularly the war in Korea and political and economic conditions in China and abroad; (2) the government's policy toward religion and the Three-Self Reform Movement; (3) the history of imperialism in China during the past hundred years. The part of the United States was especially stressed in order to cleanse the church of her pro-American leanings.

Discussion groups, composed of about sixteen members, were held every morning after the reports. Each member had to say something from his own experiences and give reactions which would support and confirm the contents of the reports they had just listened to. Every sentence spoken was recorded. The chairman of each group then handed the total record to the leader of the "Learning Meeting."

The emphasis of this indoctrination had five parts:

(1) Religion was a tool for the imperialists' aggression. They had tried to win over backward districts with a gun in one hand and a Bible in the other. They used military power to suppress, rule, and rob backward nationals. They used religion or other means to carry a cultural aggression among these suppressed nationals. Obviously, then, religious beliefs must be cleansed of the many poisonous ideas of imperialists which had lingered on.

(2) America was the most violent and cunning of the imperialist nations. America did not have the concessions of the other nations but it had had the same privileges. And worst of all, America had had complete control over all the affairs of the Kuomintang before and after World War II. In other words, the United States had exercised colonial power over China; it had openly interfered in its administration and had helped Chiang Kai-shek. America started the Korean War in order to overthrow Communist China, used germ warfare, and attacked Chinese territories north of the Yalu River. She also occupied Taiwan Province. Therefore, America was the greatest enemy of China.

(3) American imperialism, however, was a "paper tiger." For example, on the Korean battlefield America used all the latest weapons short of atomic weapons; yet the Chinese, with only out-of-date light weapons, repulsed the Americans. Therefore, what decided a war was not weapons but whether the war had the people's approval.

(4) With reference to American military bases in different parts of the world, China's view was that every American base was like a

strangling rope on America's own neck. The presence of foreign troops would certainly arouse hatred, and the behavior of American military personnel inevitably roused the people's antagonism.

(5) The Chinese people had been victorious in the anti-imperialistic struggle. They had swept away all the special privileges of foreigners in China. To complete the task, and to clean out any remaining influence of imperialism, every relationship with America —organizational, economic, and ideological—must be cut. Then China could really be free, and Christianity could be really Chinese. This was why Christianity had to be reformed. Protestants and Catholics had been used by imperialists as aggressive tools.

The reform movement of Protestants and Catholics continued the anti-imperialist struggle—it was not a denial of the freedom of worship. Each church should cut off relations with the parent church abroad and refuse to accept any overseas money. Thoughts and feelings of church workers should also be cut off from the mother church. Each one should judge the "pro-America, worship-America, fear-America" thoughts he had held in the past and produce his own patriotic thoughts. He should examine the relationship between missionaries and himself and especially their poisonous effects on his thoughts. Preachers must abide by the guidance and leadership of the government—sermons must not include anything detrimental to the general life and policy of the government.

This "Three-Self Learning Meeting" held in Peking was the initial step toward control of local churches. Peking was the center for "pilot projects"; and once the movement was tried out there, it spread to the rest of the country. All churches which had foreign connections participated, but several indigenous groups did not take part: the Shih-chia Hutung Christian Tabernacle, led by Wang Ming-tao; the Pei-hsin-ch'iao Christian Assembly, led by Wang Chen, and other Christian Assemblies (Little Flock); the En-tien Yuan (Grace Retreat Center) of Western Hills; Ling-en Yuan (Spiritual Grace Center). These groups said that their churches were governed by Chinese Christians, had no connection with foreign churches, were already self-supporting, self-governing, and self-propagating; therefore this sort of "Learning Meeting" had nothing to do with them, and there was no need for them to participate. Since the government had said "voluntary" participation, they said they did not wish to join.

Because the "thought-reform" of Chinese ministers would take time if it were to be "basic and not superficial," a permanent organization was created and given the name "the Christian Three-Self Reform Learning Committee of Peking." Thirty people from different churches were put on the committee. Its stated purpose was the political education of church members, but it was actually the first step toward a unified church organization in Peking. Through this committee the Communists increased their power over the churches.

The Three-Self Reform Learning Committee decided the methods of reforming church workers. All paid church workers had to meet once a week for political indoctrination. Catholic church members were forced to attend "learning meetings" but Protestant laymen were not. The committee, however, sent someone to each Protestant church to recruit people to propagandize other church members. By using these methods over a period of years, the Communists were able to obtain a clear picture of conditions in each church, as well as detailed knowledge of the thoughts, background, and behavior of individual church members.

The report by the "Christian layman" adds:

Then they began to take action. With their lips they continued to talk about self-government, self-support, self-propagation, while in reality they proceeded to attack the genuine self-governing, self-supporting, self-propagating churches which they regarded as "nails in the eyes" to be removed. These church organizations were organized by Chinese Christians, were entirely supported by them, and had no relationship with churches in foreign countries. They were well organized, had good fellowship, were well supported by members who were faithful in attendance and ardent in their piety. In many ways the devotion of Christians in these churches exceeded that of the churches with foreign connections. They adhered unanimously to one principle: the worship of God is the only purpose in religion, not participation in politics. When the Three Self Movement was first launched they were approached many times, but they refused to join because of that principle. Elder Yen Chia-le, a leader of the Little Flock, surrendered to the Three-Self Movement under the most difficult circumstances, but Wang Ming-tao, Wang Chen, etc., never yielded.[4]

In 1954 the first National Christian Conference was held in Peking, from July 22 to August 6. The sixteen-day conference was attended by 232 Protestant delegates from 62 different missions and bodies, and a new national committee of 139 members was elected to "guide the movement of independence in administration, support and propagation of the gospel of the Christian churches in China." Among the Committee members were Y. T. Wu, Bishop Robin T. S. Chen, Marcus Cheng, Bishop Z. T. Kaung, Wu Yi-fang and the Rev. H. H. Tsui.

Y. T. Wu, in a report to the delegates, said that the Chinese Christian churches had "basically cast off imperialist control." The patriotic movement of independence for the Chinese churches—the Christian Manifesto—signed by 1,527 leaders and members of Christian churches and organizations in 1950 had drawn in over 400,000 church members. He stressed the freedom of religious belief in new China and the unprecedented unity and "sense of solidarity" prevailing among the Chinese Christian churches. It was this unity, Wu continued, which had made possible the convening of the National Christian Conference, the first ever held by the Chinese Christians themselves.[5]

A "message of respect" to Chairman Mao was drafted and sent:

> During the past four years, through the self-government, self-supporting and self-propagating movement the Christian churches of China have basically severed their relations, both administratively and economically, with imperialism, begun to rid themselves of the influence of imperialism, and started to govern, support and preach themselves. All these successes are inseparable from your wise leadership and deep concern as well as the brilliant achievements of New China for the past several years. We are, therefore, offering our deepest gratitude on behalf of the entire Christians![6]

Finally, the meeting drafted four decisions:

(1) Under the common aim of loving the country and the Christian religion, efforts should be made to promote the great unity of all Christian churches and their members and to carry further the self-government, self-supporting, and self-propagation movement. The difference in belief, system, and ceremony observed by different churches should be mutually respected.

(2) Support the Draft Constitution of the People's Republic of China and strive together with the people of the whole nation for the construction of a socialist society, value the right of freedom of re-

ligion stipulated in the Draft Constitution, guarantee no misuse of this right for activities against the interests of the people, promote patriotism and observance of law, and fulfill the duties of a citizen.

(3) Call upon the Christians of the country for activities to safeguard the peace of the world and to firmly oppose the aggression of United States imperialism on China's territory of Taiwan.

(4) Encourage the Christians of the whole nation to seriously learn patriotism, to be thoroughly purged of the remnant influence of imperialism, and to differentiate between what is right or wrong, good or evil, to purify the churches.[7]

The conference marked the beginning of a new stage in the activities of the Three-Self Movement. For one thing, it now had a new name. In concluding his report Y. T. Wu had anounced that the original title of "Three-Self *Reform* Movement" would be dropped "for the sake of unity," and the new title would be "The Chinese Christian Three-Self *Patriotic* Movement."[8] What Wu did not describe was the widespread opposition to the interpretation given by Communist officials to the term "reform," but this was implied in a "Letter to the Churches" issued by the conference:

We know that the Three-Self Reform Movement is the concrete expression of Christian opposition to imperialism and Christian love for country; it has no purpose to change our creeds or our church organization. The word "Reform" unfortunately suggests to some people the 16th Century Reformation which did concern creeds. This has made some fellow-Christians unwilling to take part in this movement. In order to strengthen our unity, dispel unnecessary fears, show more clearly the real nature of the movement to oppose imperialism and love our country, we think it is not necessary to hold on to the original name, and so we have agreed to call it the China Christian Three-Self Patriotic Movement. We have set up a widely representative national organization, the Committee of China Christian Three-Self Patriotic Movement.

The purpose of the Three-Self Patriotic Movement is to unite the Christian Church in China in the Three-Self campaign, in positive participation in opposing imperialism and in furthering patriotic movements and world peace. We know that the purpose of "self-government" is not to unify or modify the organization of the various churches, but to get the churches to cut off all relations with imperialism, so that the churches will be ruled by Chinese Christians; the purpose of "self-support" is not to interfere in the finances of any church, but to cut off all connections with imperialistic funds, so that the responsibility for the church will be on Chinese shoulders; the purpose of "self-propagation" is not to unify or modify our creeds, but to wipe out the influence of imperialistic thought, and bring the preaching of the church into harmony with the true gospel of Jesus Christ. We should respect the differences that exist among the churches in creed, organization and ritual.[9]

The decision to change the term to "patriotic" was a tactical maneuver to win over those who were convinced that "reform" indicated interference not only in the internal affairs of the churches but also in doctrines. The word "reform" was removed to allay suspicion of the motives of government and Three-Self Movement officials. However, the push toward conformity with government policies intensified after the First National Christian Conference.

But none of this outcome was apparent from the report of Christian leaders attending the conference. At an interview with a *Hsin Hua* correspondent after the conference, four of them made glowing statements of approval for their new "freedom of unity."

The Reverend Marcus Cheng, president of the Chungking Theological Seminary, said that religious freedom had been explicitly included in both the Common Program and the Draft Constitution. He added, "Our experiences of the past four years have shown that we enjoy this freedom. It is only in a country where such religious freedom is granted that such a conference would be possible."[10]

Bishop Robin T. S. Ch'en, chairman of the House of Bishops of the Anglican Church, said that in New China Christians suffered no discrimination for their religious belief. Referring to "rumors constantly spread by the U.S. imperialists" that church leaders were being persecuted in New China Bishop Ch'en said: "The rumor has been spread that the Chinese People's Government killed 29 pastors including Pastor Wang Ming-tao. This is nonsense. I met Pastor Wang Ming-tao after I came to Peking, and a few days ago he left for Peitaiho to have a rest there. This is only one of many examples, for not a single case of persecution has happened since liberation."

What Bishop Ch'en conveniently forgot to mention was the Peking church leaders' demand for Wang Ming-tao's death earlier that year (see Chapter Eight), and his own and other leaders' reaction to Wang Ming-tao's refusal of their invitation to join the Three-Self Movement. The Christian layman already mentioned has recorded: "Instead of meeting Wang Ming-tao, who refused to receive them, they found a verse from the Bible on the blackboard at the entrance, which compared the four honourable delegates to Satan. They retreated in great anger, and no one approached Wang Ming-tao on that basis again."[11]

Bishop Z. T. Kaung, of the Chinese Methodist Church, said that religious services had been conducted freely in all Methodist churches in the country. He added, "Together with the Christians of the rest of the world, Chinese Christians would propagate the gospel of peace of Jesus Christ, and strive for world peace, so that happiness may come to all peoples in the world."

Reverend H. H. T'sui, general secretary of the General Assembly of the Church of Christ in China, said that new churches and chapels had been built under his supervision and quoted several examples. (He did not mention how many had been closed down.)

From the beginning of the Three-Self Reform Movement, Sunday worship attendance declined sharply in most churches:

The required socialistic propaganda in the ministers' sermons was distasteful to the congregations. Any breach of the socialistic line in a sermon could quickly lead to purge, so preachers were extremely cautious. Their sermons were weak, perfunctory and ineffective. So the more devoted Christians turned away and attended Wang Ming-tao's services or those of the Little Flock. Superficial members just stopped going to church. The attendance at Wang Ming-tao's Tabernacle increased greatly; on many occasions there was not even standing room in the yard. This not only aroused government resentment but also aroused hatred from the churches which the deserters left. This mounting opposition from several sectors inevitably led to Wang Ming-tao's arrest.

Communist China tolerated Wang Ming-tao for several years, although the government wanted to utilize him from the beginning. His courage, independent spirit and commitment to the truth were admired by people in all walks of life, so the Communists had to be careful in dealing with him in order to avoid unfavourable reactions in China and abroad. He was well-known internationally. It was said that when Labour Party ex-Premier Attlee visited Peking he wanted to see Wang Ming-tao as soon as he arrived.[12]

Wang Ming-tao was arrested during the "Cleaning Up Anti-Revolutionary Elements Movement" in 1955. (See Chapter Eight.)

After his arrest any member of his church who was working in a government office, hospital, or school was immediately investigated. The Three-Self Patriotic Committee recorded his "trial" and broadcast it to their own workers, but not to the general public or to church members.

During the "hundred flowers blossoming, hundred schools of thought contending" period in 1956, many of the Three-Self Movement leaders took part in condemning the government. The Chairman of the Three-Self Reform Learning Committee, Rev. Wong Tzu-chung (P. H. Wong) declared that the Communist policy of freedom of worship was a false freedom which deceived the people, and that the Three-Self Movement really intended to annihilate Christianity.[13]

Another denunciatory address was given by the Anglican Bishop K. H. Ting, president of the Nanking Union Theological Seminary, which remarkably either went unnoticed or was unpunished. The address, "Christian Theism," was made to his students on June 12, 1957; in it he laid down a forthright challenge to the materialism of Communist conviction.

He began by saying that although Christian belief is not the result of reasoning but of experience, still the Christian must be able to explain his belief intelligently. In addition the Christian must know why atheistic theories are wrong. "We must think deeper and strengthen our faith, so that when we go out to preach the truth of the gospel our words may carry weight because of their reasonableness."

Christianity does not follow the Communist line of trying to divide all systems of thought into either materialism or idealism. Although the Communists condemn idealism and approve materialism, it is impossible to completely separate the two. Even Pavlov, founder of materialist psychology, was a member of the Russian Orthodox Church. Christianity itself is neither the one nor the other and Christians should not try to defend themselves on that basis.

"Christianity . . . has of course been deeply influenced by human history, but in itself it is not the fruit of history, and the Gospel is not an ideology. The Gospel comes from the free revelation of God. This Gospel is Christ Himself, through whom all things were made." Christianity must not be reduced to another ideology in opposition to communism.

The Communist charge that "religion is the opiate of the people" was, said Bishop Ting, made against particular historical instances of religion—not against religion *per se*. It has no relevance to the question of whether or not God exists. Many things besides religion are used as opiates all the time. Suppose a man, in order to escape some family grief, chooses astronomy as his opiate; the fact that he draws calmness of mind from this activity does not mean that the sun, moon, and stars do not exist. "His subjective psychological state is one thing; the objective state of the universe is another." This is purely logical.

If people use Christianity as an opiate it is an accident, not a necessary part of Christianity. Jesus Christ himself refused any kind of drugging or opiate on the cross. To pray, "Thy will be done on earth as it is in heaven," is not an opiate but the highest religion. On John Hus's statue in Prague are carved his words, "Woe to me if I keep silent. If I do not speak out against the gravest evils, then I become an accomplice of sin and hell, and it were better had I never been born." Bishop Ting demanded: "Who dares to say that a man who talks like this has been drugged with an opiate?"

The Bishop spent some time talking about the existence of God —one can find some proof of His existence in nature, but not much. Knowledge of God comes through revelation and then nature becomes an open book.

On the Communist doctrine that every evil comes from environment, the Bishop commented that man is still off center, in spite of the better environment the Communists have brought in. Sin and social progress are two different things.

Bishop Ting then turned the tables on the atheists. Why do they not believe in God? For two reasons. One is that believing in God makes greater demands on people's lives, thinking and actions than they will accept. "Belief in God sometimes becomes an opiate, that is true. But consider how often refusal to believe in God becomes an opiate. How many men there have been since the beginning of history who have drugged themselves by a denial of God's existence, so that they could continue to sin, avoid responsibility, and stifle the reproaches of their conscience."

A second reason why people refuse to believe in God is that the Church has sinned and has not let its light shine as it should. Bishop Ting quoted Berdyaev, the Russian theologian, who said that Christians were largely to blame for the Russian revolution. They had not practiced their own principles of love and justice and brotherhood.

Bishop Ting concluded by saying that Christians must learn to live with atheists in one country, not being seduced by them but also learning how to present the Gospel to them. "The establishment of the church in a socialist country is a task that was never accomplished in all the first 19 centuries of church history. Why did the Lord give these duties to us and not to someone else? Is it because we are better? No, the Lord has His own purpose, one which we cannot fathom. But at least we know, just because our Chinese church is weak and without antecedent prestige, that we can demonstrate how the church of the Lord in weakness shows forth strength, we can show the workings of God's might and thus give glory to God. God has indeed chosen the foolish things of the world to put to shame them that are strong. This shows that the strength is from God, and not from ourselves."[14]

Following the "anti-rightist" movement of 1956, the government must have thought that the church members' political thinking had improved, in Peking at least. They were promoted from the "learning" stage to formally setting up a Three-Self Patriotic Committee, which became the official organization of the Christian Church with no denominational distinctions. The members of this Committee were chosen from the "active" ministers of different churches.[15]

Only four churches were left open in Peking from the previous sixty-five: in the East city, the Congregational church; in the West city, the Chinese Christian Church at Kang-wa Shih; in the South city, the Methodist church at Chushih K'ou; and in the North city, the Christian Assembly. Only these four churches, plus the Y.M.C.A. and the Y.W.C.A., were allowed to continue as Christian institutions in Peking, and the same pattern was followed elsewhere.

Local groups of pastors and church workers adopted resolutions in which they affirmed their loyalty to the government in a number of specific points. Copies of these resolutions were sent to the Three-Self Movement headquarters, and *Tien Feng* carried reports of several, such as that from the Yuling district as follows:

1. We will observe the five don'ts, the five musts, the five loves and the five excellencies.

The five don'ts are: We will not break the laws, we will not preach reactionary doctrine, we will not try to get people to become Christians on the plea that Christ can heal the sick, we will not invite freelance evangelists to preach in our churches, we will not attend or preach in underground services in homes.

The five musts are: We must cooperate in the government's religious policy, we must expose free-lance evangelists and underground home services, we must be economical, we must discipline our bodies, we must take part in every socialist campaign.

The five loves are: love the country, the party, socialism, the Three-Self Movement, and labor.

The five excellencies are: to improve in the openness of our thinking through criticism and self-criticism, to improve in self-reform (by destroying capitalism and establishing socialism), to improve in mutual respect (that is, between believers in different faiths, or between believers and non-believers), to improve in street activities and in relations with our neighbors, to improve in political study.

2. Besides our personal strengthening of our own political studies as pastors, we will also organize study classes for our laymen in every church.

3. We will answer the call of the government in regard to public hygiene, and in every church strictly obey the six don'ts and the three cleansings [no record of what these were].

4. We will heed the call of the government in regard to birth control, not only in our own families, but recommending it also to our laymen.

5. Every church will plant trees in every available place on our land.

6. We will wipe out illiteracy in all church members between the ages of 14 and 40 during the year 1958.[16]

With the union of the churches and the closing down of most church buildings, most pastors were out of work. Older ones were "persuaded" to retire, and younger pastors took over. Most pastors had to work at other jobs as well according to the Communist slogan "No labor—no meal"—an argument the Communists supported from the Biblical text, "he that will not work will not eat." At one point a whole series of articles in *Tien Feng* called the pastors parasitic and demanded that pastors work for society and for full economic production.[17] In Peking the young men who were healthy were sent to work at the State Farm in Han Yuan. The middle-aged who were physically fit were sent to the "Peking Husbandry Ranch." The older and weaker ministers and church workers were sent to work in the Methodist church in the East City, which had been changed into an envelope factory. Their work was pasting envelopes together.[18]

Those who were on the Three-Self Patriotic Committee did not have to take factory or farm jobs. But occasionally they would go to the farms and take other jobs for short periods, to avoid criticism. Because the people's impressions of these Three-Self Patriotic Committee pastors was so poor, most of the sincere church members stopped going to the churches, choosing rather to read the Bible and worship in their own homes.[19]

A former Presbyterian missionary in China, Rev. Samuel E. Boyle, writing in *The Bible Times* (a magazine of the Japan Christian Theological Seminary), posed the question at the end of 1958: "Is the Government-controlled Three-Self Patriotic Movement of the Protestant Church in Communist China to-day a true Church of Christ?" Then he answered: "This Church has not only distorted the essence of Christianity to conform to the State, but in its idolatrous 'Hand Over Your Hearts to the Party' campaign of 1958 the church partook of mass idolatory." He concluded of the Three-Self Patriotic Movement what Calvin said of the Church of Rome: "The form of the legitimate church is not to be found, either in any one of their congregations, or in the body at large." At the same time, God might still have "His own faithful ones" within this organization. In addition to these, of course, there were still many thousands in the "underground home services" who would have no part in the Three-Self Patriotic Movement.

A second National Conference of Chinese Christians was held in Shanghai from November 12, 1960, to January 14, 1961. A total of 319 delegates attended from 25 different provinces or independently organized cities or autonomous areas. From November 12, 1960, to January 8, 1961, it functioned as a "preparatory conference"; and the conference proper was held from January 9 to 14. During that time a report of the work of the Three-Self organization for the previous six years was read, the Three-Self Committee constitution was revised, 34 speeches were delivered and a national committee of 145 members was elected, which then elected a standing committee of 49 members consisting of a chairman, several vice-chairmen, and other delegates.

The amended constitution adopted at this conference stated in article II:

This committee is the anti-imperialist, patriotic organization of Chinese Christians. Its purposes are: Under the leadership of the Chinese Communist Party and the People's Government to unite the Christians of the country in a positive participation in socialist construction and other patriotic activities; to observe all government decrees, and assist the government in its freedom of religious belief policy; to promote in the Chinese Christian Church a complete attainment of self-government, self-support and self-propagation, and root out all imperialistic activities; to oppose imperialist aggregation, and uphold world peace.[20]

It provided for the committee of 145 to meet once a year, the Standing Committee to act for it when it was not in session, and the Conference to meet once every three years—with number of delegates and their method of selection decided by the Standing Committee.

Dr. Wu Yi-fang, vice-chairman of the Chinese Christian Three-Self Patriotic Committee gave the report on the work of the Committee from 1954 to January 1961.[21] In 1954, she said, "reactionary forces had still not been purged from the church." But in 1955, as a part of the anti-reactionary campaign, "the People's Government, on the initiative of the people and of Christians, broke up the counter-revolutionary rings headed by Wang Ming-tao and by Watchman Ni [Nee To-sheng]." At the enlarged Committee meetings of 1956 and 1957 the members present after discussion came to realize that "they must accept the leadership of the Party and walk the road of socialism." In 1958 "the Christian community made a great advance . . . in our understanding of socialism." Preachers all over the country enrolled in study programs to gain "an increased recognition" of various problems confronting the country and the people. The result was that in the past two years preachers and laymen had all been thoroughly united "with all Chinese in upholding the leadership of the Communist Party, and that we love the enlightened standpoint of socialism . . ." But Dr. Wu concluded the report by pointing out that a number of questions remained and that "although the reactionary forces within the church have received a severe blow, they have not been destroyed."

The National Conference was followed by regional conferences, the purpose of which was to report the accomplishments of the National Conference and to streamline the local organizations.

What the reform of the organizational structure of the Three-Self Patriotic Movement meant in practice can be gathered from the report of a pastor (Hsu Chi-tao, of Ch'ing Asin, South Gate Church, Shanghai), who had just done an advanced study course for pastors at Nanking Union Seminary. Giving an account of his new outlook he wrote:

The aim of the seminary to-day is to cultivate preachers and pastors who are patriotic and who love religion. The content of our study contained both religious and political courses. Through religious courses one knew that, if we have a basis of increased political consciousness and ideological understanding, the more theological knowledge we have the better.

Biblical truth and imperialist poison must be separated. Though we have taken part in political learning since liberation, our thinking is not completely free from the influence of poisonous elements. We could not readily distinguish biblical truth from imperialist poison, so we were afraid that our belief would suffer in criticizing the poison. We do not want to be the mouthpiece of imperialism any more. Some of us have become reluctant to do pulpit work. Now we know that biblical truth and imperialist poison, can and must be separated. . . . Anti-imperialist and patriotic work must be strengthened. Imperialist crimes in using religion must be further exposed. . . ."

What was emerging from the activities of the Three-Self Patriotic Movement (with the exception of a few sincere but troubled Christian leaders) was that traditional Christianity in China was in the hands of cynical Communist Party officials. These leaders were manipulating both the naïve and the anguished to further the Party's ambitions of destroying religious belief altogether. On the perimeter of the organization—or, strictly speaking, beyond its confines—there was an unknown number worshiping in "underground home services" whose presence and convictions troubled the Communist Party leaders. Slogans, threats, and mass indoctrination left them untouched and unpersuaded. Being subject neither to church organization nor to Three-Self Movement machinery, conforming in all matters of social and civil demands of government, these people could not be attacked officially by the Communist regime without its being laid open to the charge of "persecution" or "violating freedom of religion"—a course which, officially, they were reluctant to pursue.

CHAPTER SEVEN

The Communist Solution for a Catholic Church

WHEN THE COMMUNIST PARTY came to power in China in 1949, it was estimated that there were 3,000,000 Catholics, 700,000 of whom lived in rural districts. The Catholic clergy was estimated at 12,000, of whom 5,500 were foreigners.[1]

The Communist Party took much the same attitude toward the Catholic Church as it had toward Protestants in the early part of its regime. An article in the *Current Affairs Journal*[2] in 1950 gave an overall view:

From the very beginning, the activities of the Catholic Church were closely related to imperialist aggression against China. It has set up in China a large number of churches, schools, hospitals and other cultural and philanthropic institutions . . . . Some of the missionary organizations have been used by imperialists as agencies for carrying out espionage activities.

It is incumbent upon all patriotic Catholics . . . standing on the same line with all other fellow-countrymen, to disclose all the imperialist plots in utilizing religion as a means to carry out espionage work, to oppose these reactionary elements in the churches who still collude with the imperialists; to bring about step by step the self-governing, self-supporting and independent preaching of the churches; to gradually check imperialist influence and sever financial relations with foreign missions; and to make all religious activities the business of Chinese followers. Special agents who are engaged in reactionary activities and espionage shall, regardless of their nationalities, be appropriately punished by the People's Government. . . .

For the sake of public peace and order . . . no missionaries should preach the gospel outside their churches and . . . at the same time no other organizations or the public should carry out anti-religious propaganda on the premises of any church. . . . For the purpose of preaching the gospel, the churches may issue publications covering religious doctrines and teachings which, however, must not be in contravention to the Common Program.

The first measures against the Catholic Church were taken in Nanking in 1950. A Mr. Liu accused the Sacred Heart Home there with the death of his child in a letter to the Nanking *China Daily* (May 13, 1950). Eventually an article appeared in *People's China* (No. 2, 1952), which claimed to describe the conditions in the home:

New-born babies were fed half a pint of heavily watered milk a day, plus a little bean powder. Toddlers had to subsist on plain rice gruel day in and day out. . . . Tuberculosis, meningitis and other serious illnesses were left to run riot. Death took a heavy toll. Children were made to ruin their eyes on embroidery; to break their backs feeding the fowls and animals, cutting grass, planting vegetables, cleaning floors. . . . The most common form of torture was to be shut up in the "'dark room"—or cellar. Children were confined in this way for as long as twenty days without as much as a musty carrot to eat with their gruel.

The article was followed by accusations against the missionaries in charge of the home, "documented" by fifty parents.

In October, Fu Jen University in Peking was taken over by the government. In November a French doctor in the Catholic Ming Teh Middle School of Chungking was arrested, with great publicity, for allegedly misappropriating "a large quantity of medical supplies" and "trying to obstruct the patriotic activities of the students and their Youth League activities."[3]

The main attack was begun on November 30, 1950 in Szechuan. In a move similar to the organization of the Three-Self Movement, four Catholics from northern Szechuan—Father Wong Liang-tao, Hsiang Shih-chu, Wong Fu-tsu, and Sun Ke-chiang—put their names to a motion "to sever all ties with imperialism, to carry out self-government, self-support and independent preaching; to take concrete action against the United States and aid to Korea; and to struggle for the reconstruction of an independent, democratic, peaceful, unified and powerful new China."[4]

The proposal concluded:

We seek our rejuvenation with self-efforts and strive for the establishment of a new Church that is self-governing, self-supporting and self-promoting. We do not want the sanctity of the Church to be tainted by imperialism. Fellow-believers, in order to rid ourselves of the plots and aggressive designs of the imperialists, we must positively undertake concrete action. . . . We have convened a meeting here on November 30, when local authorities were also pressed to give us guidance. All members of the Church attending the meeting unanimously supported our movement. We hope that you, too, will respond to this call, to ensure the success of the movement.

More than 500 were said to have signed the statement.[5]

This proposal was also supported by Father Fan Mao-shih and 265 followers from the Anyueh district of North Szechuan in a statement issued on Christmas Day.

In January, 1951, the Government officially entered the act and invited leading Catholics to "exchange views on the Catholic Church reform movement." At the meeting Vice-Chairman Lu Ting-yi of the government administration delivered a speech in which he spoke of the call to reform the Catholic church as "an entirely proper patriotic action." Lu went on to urge Chinese Catholics "to unite, to sever all relations with imperialism, and turn the Chinese Catholic Church into a religious organization operated by the Chinese themselves."

He was followed by Chou En-lai, who stated: "The reform movement initiated by the religious circles should be promoted. The people's government will give it aid and support. This is a patriotic movement of the religious circles. To love one's fatherland is the duty of all, including Catholics."[6]

Immediately, pressure to conform to the government decree was exerted on all Catholic leaders and laymen. The defiance of Father John Tung in Chungking in June, 1951, has already been recorded (in Chapter Three). In August of that same year another priest, Father Beda Chang, was imprisoned. Before his arrest he had been chosen by the Communist authorities as leader of the "Independent Church." But when he would not cooperate, he was imprisoned and tortured to death. When news of his death became known, police had to be called in from neighboring cities to prevent riots.

> Upon Father Beda Chang's death, all churches in the whole diocese of Shanghai were packed at the special Masses, and many wept publicly. . . . It was decided by Bishop Ignatius Kung of Shanghai that all Catholics in the city should mourn for Father Chang by wearing a white flower for a week. But the people with white flowers could be seen in churches and schools even after two or three weeks had elapsed.[7]

The martyrdoms of Father John Tung and Father Beda Chang created considerable tension in Catholic circles. Until these events, some Catholic leaders were prepared to go along with the idea of an independent Chinese Catholic Church. Now it was clear that the issue was either martyrdom or betrayal of the Church, and it was no longer possible to believe that only foreign missionaries were being removed from the country.

By the end of 1952, 1,046 priests, brothers, and sisters had been expelled from China, leaving 787 foreign Catholic missionaries still in the country—524 priests, 210 nuns, and 53 brothers. Two archbishops and two bishops had died in prison, 14 more were in prison, 3 were under house arrest, and 43 had been expelled. In 1951, 19 Chinese priests had been killed or had died in prison, and an unknown number of Chinese lay and religious had died. In 1953 there were still over 300 Chinese priests imprisoned.[8]

By 1953 three Catholic universities, 189 secondary schools, 2,011 primary schools, and 2,243 prayer schools involving 30,000 students had been taken over or closed down. All but one of the 32 Catholic presses had been confiscated by the government and closed down, or else switched to publishing secular material.

The period 1950-53 was a difficult one for the Catholic Church in China. A report in 1953 recorded:

> About the existence of the Church in the hearts of the Chinese clergy

and laity there is no question, it is hardy and loyal, but as for the exterior and organized Church there is reason for us to halt a moment and take stock of the situation. In some dioceses there are very few Chinese priests and often in these as well as in the ones where they are more numerous, half or more of them are in prison or under house arrest; in another eight out of eighteen, and in a third there are eight out of ten in jail. In other dioceses where there are still foreign missionaries, all of them are either under house arrest or in jail. . . .

. . . However we may say to-day that the Independent Church Movement has been a sorry fiasco. In its early stages, under a patriotic smokescreen of propaganda, it enjoyed a bit of support. At that point its true nature and import were not clear to either the clergy or lay people. By the movement, the Communists hoped to split the Chinese Catholics away from the foreign missionaries and to cut one by one the ties of the Catholic Church in China with Rome. Once the true nature of the Independent Church became known, namely that it meant *schism*, the Chinese clergy, religious and lay Catholics shunned it like a man with leprosy. At the present writing there are about 77 dioceses in which the clergy are completely free from any taint of "progressivism." In many others, due to the personnel, there is no question of it. . . .⁹

Obviously, this state of affairs was not what the Communist leaders in Peking wanted. In 1951 they had tried to get the Catholic Church to join the Three-Self Movement. Marcus Cheng had been given the task of trying to accomplish this, but had been unable to.¹⁰ They particularly did not want a church with any relationship or ties to a foreign power. However, it was not time for a major confrontation yet. So between 1953 and 1955 Catholics were comparatively free from persecutions and pressures while the government dealt with the problem of the Protestants. But in 1955 the authorities were ready to attempt once more a settlement of the Catholic question.

The year 1955 seemed to be the year when the Communists felt secure enough to attack the most outspoken and popular of their critics. Wang Ming-tao, the Protestant conservative preacher, was arrested in Peking in July 1955 (see Chapter Eight). Their principal target was Bishop Ignatius Kung Ping-mei, the strongest opponent of the "Patriotic Catholic Independent Church" movement; and Shanghai, the Bishop's diocese, was the main stronghold of opposition to the movement. He was arrested on September 8 with a large number of other priests and Catholic laymen. The arrests were followed by an organized press campaign against "the Kung Ping-mei counter-revolutionary clique."

Bishop Kung was accused of heading a vast network of "counter-revolutionary agents" throughout China in order to conspire against the government. Dr. Yang Shih-ta, vice-president of the Catholic Association of Shanghai, described the arrests to the People's Political Consultative Conference in Peking on February 7, 1956, as a popular movement against the conspiracy—"the last imperialist bastion disguised under the cloak of religion was annihilated by the arm of the people." He went on: "Imperialist agents, members of the Kung Ping-mei counter-revolutionary clique, were arrested. We have seen how these agents spread among the diocese of China. As soon as the counter-revolutionary movement was launched in 1955, we arrested one after another, like a string of crabs, all counter-revolutionaries who were connected with Kung Ping-mei in hiding in Catholic churches in different parts of China."[11]

A great deal of evidence was brought against Bishop Kung, including the publication of a letter, purportedly signed by seventy-five Shanghai priests, denouncing his activities. Later, however, the authenticity of this document was challenged when several of the priests denied having signed the letter.[12]

The accusations against "the Kung Ping-mei counter-revolutionary clique," according to the Shanghai *Sin Wen Jih Pao* (September 14, 1955), were:

Investigation and seized evidence proved that this batch of counter-revolutionaries, who had long been under the cultivation of the Kung Ping-mei counter-revolutionary clique, had frantic counter-revolutionary ambitions. They had not only laid down their counter-revolutionary rules, regulations, systems and organization, but had also drawn up a set of clearly stipulated counter-revolutionary principles. Their ultimate objective was to assist in the restoration of the counter-revolutionary regime and imperialist domination of the whole world. In order to realize their principle and attain their aim, they laid down ten important steps, including the formation of counter-revolutionary troops, the organization of armed revolts, and the overthrow of the People's Government.

In spite of the serious charges against Bishop Kung, the Communists did not have an immediate public trial for him, but kept him in prison. Then suddenly, on March 17, 1960, it was announced that Bishop Kung and thirteen other members of the Chinese Catholic Church had been convicted at public trials in Shanghai on March 16-17 and sentenced to prison terms ranging from five years to life.

Bishop Kung's arrest was the beginning of a campaign to eliminate all opposition to the proposed Independent Catholic Church, and a concurrent campaign to win Chinese Catholics to the National Catholic Patriotic Association (the Catholic version of the Three-Self Movement). Articles in the newspapers maintained that the contradictions between the Catholic Church and the Communist Party were not antagonistic but "nonantagonistic contradictions." It was argued that "counterrevolutionaries" had existed and continued to exist in the Church, but that basically the contradiction now had been correctly solved.

The articles quoted Mao Tse-tung's work *On Contradiction*. Contradictions, he said, existed in the very essence of things. Opposites may temporarily be united but it is a conditional, transitory, relative unity. Struggle between them, however, is universal and absolute. Antagonism within the contradiction is a form of struggle within the contradiction. It is only when the contradiction has developed to a certain stage that unity of opposites ceases and they assume the form of open antagonism—they struggle and a new thing is produced. Contradiction and struggle are universal and absolute, but the forms of struggle differ according to the differences in the nature of the contradictions. Some contradictions are antagonistic in nature, while others are nonantagonistic. Even if the contradictions are nonantagonistic, however, while they coexist the struggle between them is ceaseless. When the struggle reaches a certain stage, the contradiction becomes antagonistic and the struggle grows acute.

As applied to the Catholic religion or to religion in general, the contradiction between religion and atheism, between idealism and materialism, is not denied. The two opposites are struggling within coexistence, and are nonantagonistic. At a certain stage in development, however—when the economic and class basis of religion is destroyed—the struggle of the opposites will become antagonistic and religion will disappear. In the meantime, since the contradiction is nonantagonistic, Communists would, within the framework of a united front, struggle with religious elements by means of "persuasion" and "education." The struggle, or resistance of the religious elements, would be controlled through the policy of suppressing counterrevolutionaries—the result of antagonistic contradiction which "justifies" the use of force.[13]

On August 3, 1957, the Peking *Jen Min Jih Pao* (*People's Daily*) reported the discussions which had just taken place at the National Conference of Catholics "attended by 241 archbishops, bishops, priests, and lay Catholics from over 100 dioceses in the whole country." The conference had discussed "two roads," the problem of elimination of counterrevolutionaries within the church, the problem of the anti-imperialist and patriotic movement of Chinese Catholics, and the relation between the Chinese Catholic Church and the Vatican as well as the question of religious policies.

The question of relation between the Chinese Catholic Church and the Vatican was one of the most important items on the agenda. The editorial in the *Jen Min Jih Pao* said:

Since the founding of the Chinese People's Republic, the Vatican has issued a stream of secret "decrees" and orders to Chinese Catholics. For instance, on January 1, 1952, it issued a "Decree to the Chinese Catholics" and on October 7, 1954, issued a "Decree to the Chinese Archbishops, bishops of the diocese and lay Catholics" aimed at inciting the Chinese Catholics to rise against the People's Government and the Communist Party and disrupting the cause of socialism in China.

When the Chinese Catholics began their patriotic movement against imperialism the Vatican tried to stop it and break it up by threatening patriotic clergy and laity with "schism," "suspension" and "excommunication." This brought home to patriotic Catholics the fact that the Vatican had clearly gone beyond the limits of religion. It was doing reactionary work in the guise of religion, interfering in China's internal matters, violating her sovereignty and actually transgressing against the Chinese Catholics' freedom of religious belief. Can this be tolerated?

The answer to the last question was, of course, "no." As a result of this conference, a Congress of Catholics in Szechuan was held from October 28 to December 15, 1957. One hundred and forty-nine bishops, archbishops, vice-bishops, priests, and laymen met to discuss "the problem of independence and self-government of the Chinese Catholic Church and the appointment of bishops by ourselves." They adopted a resolution to this effect and also decided "to set up a Preparatory Committee for the Catholic Patriotic Association of Szechuan." This resolution was not adopted without considerable opposition from several "rightists."[14]

By the middle of March, 1958, the N.C.P.A. was ready for the official break with the Vatican. At that time Tung Kuang-Ching was elected Archbishop of Hankow and Yuan Weu-hua, Bishop of Wuchang. The election was said to have been held "in the spirit of the resolution on the independent administration of the Church adopted by the second session of the First Wuhan Municipal Representative Conference of Catholics."

In April, eighty-two Catholic priests and representatives of the church in Peking and Shanghai, twenty provinces, and one autonomous region came to Hankow for the consecration of the two bishops-elect.[15]

When the Vatican "refused to confirm the two bishops-elect and threatened them and the consecrating bishops with excommunication,"[16] the representatives at the consecration "unanimously" adopted a protest against the Vatican.

The protest declared:

From historical facts and personal experiences, we have realized that the Vatican has considerably used the Catholic Church in China as an instrument of aggression for imperialism. For a long period, the bishopric in various dioceses in China has been usurped by imperialist elements. The latter, operating under cover of the cloak of religion, have carried out espionage activities in China and collected information on military, political and economic affairs. . . . On the other hand, the Vatican issued time and again "circulars" and "orders" in the name of God, forcing us to oppose our beloved motherland, and coercing Chinese Catholics to "shed blood" and become "martyrs" for the sake of its political intrigues. The Vatican also took advantage of and used "excommunication" and other religious measures to persecute and deal blows to the leaders of the Catholic clergy and laymen remaining firm in their patriotic stand and adhering to the principles of justice."

The protest then declared that "all reactionary orders" and "supreme excommunications" issued and enforced by the Vatican in the name of religion were "worthless and invalid," and affirmed the right of the Chinese Catholic Church to elect their own bishops, because "the voice of the people is the voice of God."[18]

The Catholic leaders who still resisted the pressures to join or approve the formation of the N. C. P. A. were singled out for public attack. One of the most prominent was Monseigneur Teng Yi-ming, Bishop of Canton. These attacks were followed by others on "rightist Catholic elements" throughout the country and continued through the sudden "trial" and imprisonment of Bishop Ignatius Kung Ping-mei and Bishop James Walsh in March 1960.

Bishop Walsh was accused of "organizing spies, counterrevolutionaries and criminal activities" and taking "the leadership of the reactionary organizations such as 'Hua Ming News Agency' and 'Legion of Mary' which were directly under the 'Central Bureau of Catholics.' " Through these organizations he and other leaders were in a position to collect military, political, and economic information and to instigate Catholics to fight against the Communist Party and the People's Government.[19]

By the end of 1961 the government was in control of both Catholic and Protestant wings of the Christian church in China through the two puppet organizations of the National Catholic Patriotic Association and the Three-Self Patriotic Movement. In an article on "A Correct Understanding and Implementation of the Party Policy Concerning Freedom of Religious Belief" in the spring of 1962, Chang Chih-i claimed:

The Party policy of freedom in religious belief is a thorough policy covering all aspects. The absolute majority of professional men of religion have a clear knowledge of it since the mass campaign of democratically reforming the religious systems. . . .

Other people think that after democratically reforming the religious systems, further implementation of the Party policy of freedom in religious belief is no longer necessary. This thought is neither practical nor correct. They should know that a religion is not produced and developed by itself and by accident but has its roots deep in the society and human knowledge.[20]

In other words, there was still reforming to be done. Even though both Catholic and Protestant churches had been "reformed"—although hardly "democratically"—the Communist leaders in Peking were aware of an unreformed remnant. There still remained a Christian witness in China that was not "Western-orientated," "imperialist," or "traitorous" but was national in character, alive and dynamic, and every bit as passionately committed in its belief and loyalties as the atheistic Communist Party of China.

CHAPTER EIGHT

The "Nonconformists" in Communist China

THOUGH THE COMMUNISTS BELIEVED that theistic religion must be abolished eventually, there were practical considerations which made them hesitate to eliminate it forcibly. Hence, the necessity for the variety of measures which have been noted in previous chapters.

The traditional weakness of institutional religion in China was one explanation for the relatively optimistic and even benign views which the Chinese Communists at first adopted toward religion in their country. C. K. Yang in his book, *Religion in Chinese Society,* has described institutional religion as it emerged in the modern period:

As an organized body, modern institutional religion had a very small priesthood, divided into minute units of two or three units each, largely unconnected with each other. It had barely enough financial resources for subsistence for this scanty personnel. It was deprived of the support of an organized laity. . . . It did not participate in various organized aspects of community life such as charity, education, and the enforcement of moral discipline. There was no powerful centralized priesthood to dominate religious life or to direct operation of the secular social institutions.[1]

When the Communists came to power, therefore, they were not confronted with traditional or indigenous religious institutions which could have offered any effective organized resistance, in the Russian or East European sense. The Chinese attitude to religion was stated in this way:

Like anything else, religion will undergo the same process of birth, growth and extinction. . . . As his [man's] political consciousness and cultural level soar, there will inevitably be fewer and fewer people interested in religion. People gradually will become aware of the natural and social laws of development and unravel their mystery, no longer reading natural and social forces as strange and terrible. Moreover, they will be capable of grasping the natural and social laws of development, employing them to save mankind and obliterating mankind's enslaved status in the face of such forces. By that time people will no longer believe in the presence of a creator or God in the unfathomable beyond.[2]

Religion, according to the Chinese Communists, has two roots, "social" and "cognitive."[3] The social roots of religion are found in the class struggle. The exploiting classes use religion to drain the masses of their revolutionary energy, telling them that their miserable life on earth is only a brief interval on the road to eternal happiness in the heavenly kingdom—in other words, as an opiate.

The "cognitive" roots of religion come from poverty or economic backwardness, and failure to conquer the forces directing nature and society. However, as man is more and more able to grasp and use the objective laws which govern his existence, then his need for religious faith dwindles. This is called ideological awareness. Ideally, when this awareness reaches a certain level, with his economic well-being, he will finally be freed from religious influences.

These theories, however, somehow failed to be substantiated by developments in China. Once the merely nominal adherents of the Christian churches had been eliminated by charges of "crimes against the people," by intimidation, by compromise, or by submissive acceptance of official policy, there still was left a formidable core. These might be few in numbers in relation to the millions in China, but they were dedicated believers, they were model citizens, they were "socially productive units," they attended the necessary political instruction meetings—and they were ready to defy the government to worship as they believed, they were ready to be imprisoned for their convictions, they were ready to die for their faith. They represented a dangerous nucleus that must be suppressed at all costs.

No formal campaign was launched against them; but official word must have been passed to the Three-Self Movement, for new pressures were initiated against all "committed" Christians.

According to an eyewitness account by Joseph N. C. Kung, nephew of the Catholic Bishop Ignatius Kung of Shanghai:

The Communists used every possible method, including murder and jailing, to subdue those who resisted them. They imprisoned groups of outstanding Catholics who had kept in touch with the Church authorities. But the more they killed, the more converts were baptized. After many arrests the Communists attempted to nullify the work of the Catholic action groups by mixing a few turncoats in with them. The Church in turn strengthened herself by forming a Youth Front which included numerous active groups of the Legion of Mary. The Youth Front and the Legion of Mary then collaborated openly in the defense of the Church. They became, as it were, a bulwark protecting and inspiring the Catholic youth in China.[4]

The Communists then singled out for special attention the Legion of Mary. By the end of 1953, 70 of them had died. There were approximately 5,300 Catholic missionaries in China in 1950; by 1952 only some 1,500 remained, many of these in prison. "Others had been beheaded, bayoneted, burned alive, had their heads crushed between stones, had been dragged and beaten by mobs until they died."[5]

But the removal of the priests and missionaries, the dissolving of the organizational structure and the destruction of buildings, were not sufficient to eliminate the commitment of Christians to their faith. The 1953 report that told of the closing of schools went on to add:

In schools and at home, in the jobs, in their neighbourhood gatherings, in general meetings and small discussion groups, they are relentlessly forced to declare and reveal themselves and they do it uncompromisingly and with courage, bringing everything back to the one foundation of religion. . . . Even though deprived of their pastors by exile, prison or house arrest and often even deprived of their churches, they will put together enough money to rent a hall or room and obtain a priest who has been forced to live at home or with a family for the Sunday Mass. They have devised ingenious ways of receiving the Sacraments from imprisoned priests or those in hiding. Wherever the Catholic lay people have shown any weakness or wavering it is not a choice of open apostasy but rather of temporarily submitting until they can find a way out. They would prefer to choose open martyrdom. Actually there are many lay Catholic heroes and martyrs but we don't receive the same detailed information on them that we do on the priests and religious.[6]

Throughout 1953 and 1954 the pressures mounted against Catholics and the fundamentalist indigenous groups. A Catholic missionary who had been imprisoned and then expelled from the country said on his arrival in Hong Kong:

We have seen the Church in China, truly the Church and truly Chinese, and we know that she cannot die. The blood of the martyrs is the seed of the Church and our Catholic youth have understood that it is their blood, their lives that count. There is no narrow nationalism in their attitude; they are too Catholic for that. . . . They claim the right of suffering for Christ themselves in their own land, and in that, as in the depth of their Catholic living, it is clear that even in these young souls, the Church in China has reached maturity and achieved her birthright.[7]

How this was being done by the committed Christians, who were not leaders in their communities but simply members of congregations, can be seen from the following account.

On the night of June 15, 1953, the police raided the homes of six priests, several pastors and the Jesuit Fathers of Zikawei [Shanghai]. Several Jesuits were immediately taken to jail, others were put under house arrest. Thousands of Catholics gathered at the square of Zikawei and knelt to say the rosary, opposite the house where these priests were under Communist guard. The people ignored the machine-guns which were pointed at them. Still more and more Catholics gathered, their voices reciting the rosary in louder and louder unison with the prayers of the imprisoned priests. What a magnificent scene it was: soldiers, machine-guns, priests under guard, people at the rosary![8]

The Communist leaders were obviously in a quandary. If for every few local priests or pastors arrested, several thousand members of churches were to be fired with visions of self-sacrifice and martyrdom, the measures were self-defeating. As the *New York Times* (May 14, 1956) put it:

One example of how the persecutors are defeating themselves in Red China is the recent mock trial of Bishop Ignatius Kung (Kung Pin-mei) of Shanghai. To each humiliating accusation a group of 4,000 persons cried out: "Long live our Bishop!" The trial had to be stopped and the Bishop dragged off to prison again.

Yet the Communist leaders, equally obviously, could not leave such a dedicated nucleus of Christian believers untouched and free to spread their doctrines. In Peking, Wang Ming-tao was still thundering out his opposition to the liberal, government-controlled Three-Self Movement and the government itself, and several hundred students met there annually from different parts of the country. In Shanghai one large church arranged for a rota of sixty members to spend one hour daily, six at a time, from 8 A.M. to 6 P.M. in an unbroken chain of prayer. In 1955 the Christian Workers Mission reported that their workers in Inner Mongolia, Sinkiang, the Tibetan border, and West China were seeing many converts and building new churches. The demand for Christian literature was overwhelming.[9]

Early in 1955 the Communist leaders must have come to the conclusion that they would have to resort to strong measures if this "spiritual" opposition was not to get out of hand. But from subsequent events they must have decided on compromise measures; namely, to use intimidation tactics against the outstanding leaders of the various Christian organizations and groups. Starting with national figures, they would move to regional and then local leaders; with Catholics, from bishops to priests to laymen; with Protestants, from pastors to elders to laymen.

The key Protestant figure was Wang Ming-tao. Early in 1954, there had been rumors in different parts of China, later filtering into Hong Kong, that he had been arrested, imprisoned, and even executed. From subsequent accounts it has been possible to piece together what actually took place.[10]

It appears that sometime in September, 1954, the Three-Self Movement ordered all churches and Christian organizations in Peking to send delegates to an "accusation" meeting at which Wang Ming-tao was to be the victim. The charges against him were: (1) he was not in sympathy with the government; (2) he refused to take part in the Three-Self Movement; (3) his preaching was "individual-istic" and "its purpose not clear."

When the meeting began there was considerable confusion. Many rose to denounce Wang Ming-tao; many others tried to leave the proceedings in protest but were prevented from doing so. Following the accusations someone demanded that he should be put to death; but when the proposal was put to the vote, only about a quarter of those present were in favor. Throughout the meeting Wang Ming-tao sat quietly on the platform, his eyes turned toward the ceiling, never uttering a word. Many were weeping openly. The meeting was incon-clusive and no action was taken.

Several days after the meeting the student organization in Peking began an "Oppose the Persecution of Wang Ming-tao" campaign. This spread rapidly and was supported by Peking churches and organizations, then by other churches in other cities until it was publicized all over China. Prior to the accusation meeting Wang Ming-tao had not been preaching, but was leading prayer meetings in his home and writing extensively, not only for his own *Spiritual Food Quarterly,* but also books and pamphlets. He had to set up his own type and print his own magazines and books because no printer was willing to do it.

He resumed preaching late in 1954 to larger crowds than ever. In January, 1955, he preached to the largest-attended winter meet-ings he had ever had. Hundreds stood outside the church building in the bitter cold to listen to the address from the loudspeakers. Many conversions were reported.

In May, Three-Self Movement leaders decided to make one last effort to win over Wang Ming-tao. Six of the most prominent went to see Wang Ming-tao at his home—but he refused to meet them. At that time the well-known Communist writer, Hu Feng, had been expelled from the Party, and both Wang Ming-tao and Hu Feng were the subjects of attacks in all the leading religious and secular press circles.

The Three-Self Movement's magazine, *Tien Feng,* gave lists of "accusation meetings" held throughout the country to denounce Wang Ming-tao. On July 31, 1955, it published a strong article against Wang Ming-tao, listing all his "crimes." His main crime was being unpatriotic, having "no feeling for the People, for he has a heart of lead. . . . This attitude of political hatred naturally destroys the 'Oppose Imperialism—Love One's Country Movement.' "

The article was most likely the result of a special meeting held in Hankow on July 25. This was the "Wuhan Leadership Studies Group"—forty-nine men who met to accuse Wang Ming-tao.

During this time, Wang Ming-tao held two weeks of special meetings which, like the ones in winter, were completely packed, with overflowing crowds listening outside. In 1954 he had published a powerful indictment of the Three-Self Movement entitled "Betraying the Son of Man with a Kiss"; on August 7 he preached another sermon on the theme: "They in This Manner Betrayed Jesus." It was a pointed reference to what he was convinced was the great betrayal of Christ by the Three-Self Movement.

After the sermon he distributed to his congregation copies of a powerfully worded pamphlet entitled "We Because of Our Faith." In it he again pointed out the issues as he saw them—belief vs. disbelief in the Scriptures and the basic doctrines of the faith.

"We will not unite," he wrote, "with unbelievers, and we will never join any of their organizations. . . . We shall make whatever sacrifice is required of us in being faithful to God. The twisting of the Word and the consequent falsehoods cannot intimidate us."

This was his last public sermon. The Three-Self Movement and the government now felt confident enough to move against him. In the early hours of the morning of August 8, Wang Ming-tao and his wife were awakened, tied up, and taken off to jail with eighteen student members of his congregation. All were charged with resistance to the government.

In the year before his arrest Wang Ming-tao wrote a number of articles for his *Spiritual Food Quarterly*. One, entitled "Truth or Poison," analyzed the Communist charge that the Chinese church had been poisoned by the imperialist teaching of the founding missionaries and the truth of the gospel had been perverted.

Wang Ming-tao himself tried to view the missionaries dispassionately. He had not agreed with much of missionary work, and felt that Christianity in China tended generally to be more Western than spiritual. Leslie Lyall said of him, "Few Chinese Christian leaders have been so independent of foreign missions, or have been so severely critical of their mistakes and shortcomings. . . . at the same time few have shown such personal regard and Christian love for individual missionaries."[11]

He was neither anti-Western nor narrowly chauvinistic; he was deeply committed to truth and integrity. So he turned on the Three-Self Movement, accusing them of not being explicit and truthful about the alleged "poisonous activities." The real poisons that the Communists were afraid of were:

1. Emphasizing the distinction between Christians and atheists;
2. Advocating the principle, "Be not unequally together with unbelievers";
3. Attacking other Christians with differing beliefs.

These are Scriptural principles, which the Communists wanted Christians to abandon. Wang Ming-tao went on to say that those who attacked these principles were really helping the atheistic masters to destroy the true gospel. The Communists were aware that they could not destroy the gospel by open persecution or merely eliminate it by government decree; they were trying an underhanded approach—getting anti-Christian propaganda *inside* the Church to weaken and nullify the Christians' faith. The Communists knew that a Church with only an outward form and ritual but no inner life or convictions was powerless. "If the Church should ever be reduced to such a state, though there were Sunday services and other religious formalities, she would in fact have already been liquidated."

Wang Ming-tao concluded:

In conclusion, a word to the saints. In the Scriptures there is nothing but the pure truth of God, without any "imperialist poison." . . . We must go on believing and preaching it. Nobody can interfere with us and nobody can forbid us to do this. We are ready to pay any price to preserve the Word of God and we are equally willing to sacrifice anything in order to preach the Word of God. . . .

Dear brothers and sisters, let us be strong through the mighty power of the Lord! Let us profess our faith with courage and spread the Gospel with zeal! Let us be prepared to be faithful to the Lord at any cost! Our God is almighty and He will keep all those who are faithful to Him. Our Lord is the Lord of victory, who will lead us from victory unto victory. Now is the time for us to stand up and fight for His holy name, for His Gospel and for His church. Don't be cowards! Don't be weary! Don't give way! Don't compromise! The battle is indeed furious and the battlefield certainly full of dangers; but God's glory will be manifest there. He will honor them who honor Him. He will glorify those who glorify Him. Hark! The trumpet has been blown! Look, The victory is in sight! My dear brothers and sisters, let us follow in the steps of the Lord and, holding aloft His banner, go forward courageously for His Gospel's sake.[12]

Wang Ming-tao was sentenced without trial to fifteen years' imprisonment, but was released after serving thirteen months. During his term of imprisonment two Communist agents were with him constantly arguing and debating with him in order to "reform his thoughts." He was released early because he had submitted to reform, but his health was broken and he was not able to work. As evidence of his "reform" he read a self-examination paper at a public meeting called to welcome his release. In it he admitted to being "a counter-revolutionary offender," and to "sabotaging various government plans and the Socialist reconstruction movement."

As a result of the patient attitude shown by the Government and the re-education given me I have come to realize my errors. I have been accorded generous treatment by the Government and have been saved from the abyss of crime. For this my heart is full of gratitude.[13]

Wang Ming-tao was not only broken in body; he was broken in mind as well. He was severely depressed and accused himself of being first Judas, then Peter.

Later both he and his wife repudiated his "confession" saying it was not his own statement and did not contain his true convictions. He was again arrested and imprisoned and then put under home arrest. Some time after his return to prison a leader of the Three-Self Movement said that Wang Ming-tao was imprisoned because he engaged in espionage. But as Dr. Francis Price Jones notes, this was obvious nonsense, for not even in the statement attributed to him was there any mention of political offenses.[14]

Dr. Jones has also said that a hymn that came out of Peking in 1953, which attracted considerable attention in the United States and is included in several collections of hymns, was possibly written by Wang Ming-tao. The hymn challenges the Communist claim that "labor creates everything" and affirms that God is not only creator but love as well[15] (see Appendix IV).

Other indigenous leaders were also arrested and imprisoned on equally ludicrous charges. Watchman Nee of the influential Christian Assemblies, it has already been noted, was arrested in 1952 and sentenced to fifteen years' imprisonment on charges of being a capitalist and "multiple adulterer" (he was said to have seduced over a hundred women). On January 21, 1956, the four elders who had continued the pastoral duties, with some other twenty-six leaders in the Shanghai area, were arrested.

In their case, the Government was not afraid to have a public trial. On January 30, 2,500 prominent Christians, mostly from the Christian Assemblies, were ordered to attend a mass denunciation meeting in Shanghai, conducted by two prominent Communists— the Chairman of the Shanghai Religious Affairs Bureau, and the vice-mayor of Shanghai. The latter gave the main speech in which he made the expected accusations that these men were arrested because they were counterrevolutionaries. While the Christian Assemblies was not actually a counterrevolutionary organization, some of its members were counterrevolutionaries. And although there was complete religious freedom, still the People's Government would not stand for the use of religion to obstruct the economy or to cover up any kind of activity against the revolution. So every counterrevolutionary in the Christian Assemblies would be rooted out.[16]

The campaign against the Christian Assemblies was carried from Shanghai to other cities, and so many leaders were arrested that the character of the movement was completely changed. The leaders were charged with "carrying on destructive activities, breaking down government policies and control movements, scattering reactionary words and counter-revolutionary rumors, instilling fear in the hearts of church members, poisoning the minds of youth, and destroying the unity of the Christian church in opposing imperialism and in love for country and church."[17]

After the members of the Christian Assemblies had been "re-educated" and their thoughts "reformed," they were "permitted" to join the Three-Self Patriotic Movement. They were formally admitted to the movement on April 15, 1956.[18]

The founder of the Jesus Family, Ching Tien-ying, also had been arrested in 1952 for being dictatorial and an adulterer. After his arrest the many communities of the Jesus Family were reorganized by Three-Self leaders into regular churches, doing away with communal living and working. After the campaign against the Jesus Family, a number of Three-Self leaders had to write articles retracting their earlier praise of the communities as Christian examples of Communist principles. As Francis Price Jones notes, the real reason for Ching Tien-ying's arrest was not immoral conduct (a false charge), but that in a Communist state only one pattern of communal living and only one dictatorship is allowed.[19]

Isaac Wei, son of the founder of the "True Jesus" Church had been arrested in 1951 (see Chapter Five). Some time later, several leaders from the church's headquarters in Wuhan were imprisoned on charges that their faith healing, speaking in tongues, and other practices were "unscientific" and harmful.[20]

The result of these tactics was that in 1956 the Three-Self Patriotic Movement could claim to represent most, if not all, of the churches of China. At the Second National Conference of the movement, held in Peking March 15-23, 1956, 269 delegates came from every province in China. There were representatives from the churches of Wang Ming-tao and Watchman Nee and other evangelical movements which had formerly opposed the movement. There were also four guests from overseas: Professor Joseph Hromadka of Czechoslovakia, Bishop Peter Jonas of Hungary, Dr. Gustav Nystrom of Sweden, and Bishop Rajah Manikam of India. All four made speeches praising the Three-Self Movement, and Bishop Manikam expressed the view that other churches could learn lessons from it.[21]

Y. T. Wu made a long report to the conference on the accomplishments of the movement from 1954-1956. Twenty-two new regions had been organized and admitted to the movement, making a total of 197. There had been retreats and evangelistic crusades in some of the larger cities. Although he reported that theological schools were open and students were applying, Wu gave no figures. And there was a need for more Christian workers, he said. There was also need for the churches to be self-supporting and self-propagating, and for Chinese Christian literature. And he called on all Christians to support the government and to participate in all government programs.[22]

A conference letter sent out to all Chinese Christians spoke of the recent successful drive to root out imperialism from the church, and likened it to the purification of the Temple by Christ. The result was that there was now complete unity of the churches in the Three-Self Movement; the counterrevolutionaries who were wearing the hat of "faith" had been uncovered and arrested, "and the deluded brothers and sisters have come to a realization of the true situation."[23]

Toward the end of 1956—in November—the first free world church leaders visited Communist-controlled China. This was an Australian delegation of eight Anglicans, led by Archbishop Howard W. K. Mowll. In Peking Francis James of the delegation interviewed Ho Chen-hsiang, the director of the Religious Affairs Bureau. Ho insisted that the government was open to criticism and that it encouraged the church "in a constructive way."

"If all is as you say," Mr. James replied, "then why are there so many Christian leaders still in prison? To my certain knowledge there are four Roman Catholic Bishops and three Protestants. And Wang Ming-tao and our own Bishop Kimber Den have only just been released from jail. If that is not religious persecution what is it?"

The reply was that these men had committed political offenses and were not imprisoned due to religious persecution.[24]

Roman Catholics in China were undergoing similar persecution. In September, 1956, there were twenty-four foreign missionaries still in China—Bishop James Walsh, three priests with limited freedom, nine priests in prison, and eleven Franciscan sisters.[25] In all, 166 missionaries had been killed or had died in prison—127 Chinese and 39 foreign. And 346 foreign missionaries had been imprisoned from two months to four years. There was no figure known for the Chinese priests imprisoned.[26] It was estimated, however, that by 1954, between seven hundred and eight hundred Chinese priests had lost their lives in the persecution.[27]

As the government had selected Watchman Nee and Wang Ming-tao as representative Protestant leaders, so they selected Bishop Walsh and Bishop Ignatius Kung as representative Catholic leaders. Bishop Kung was arrested with his vicar general, Monseigneur Silvester Tsu, and a large number of his clergy and laymen in Shanghai during September, 1955 (see Chapter Seven). From there the campaign spread throughout China. One report stated:

More and more it emerges as a final concentrated effort to break the power of the Catholic Church in China once and for all, using as a pretext the current counter-revolutionary campaign. . . . Following the usual pattern, mass meetings of "loyal" Catholics have been organized to denounce "traitorous" Catholic priests, nuns and prominent Catholic laymen. 30,000 Catholics attended one such meeting in Shanghai.[28]

Bishop Walsh, like a number of other missionaries, had refused to leave China when the Communists took over. He never wavered from his determination to stay. When he was put under military guard—which amounted to house arrest—and the word got out to foreign newspapers, he received many telephone calls from Hong Kong, Manila, and even Tokyo. At first he accepted them; but later he asked that people stop phoning. He was afraid that whatever he said might be reported out of context, or exaggerated, and be dangerous to other missionaries or the church in China.

The Bishop's refusal to leave China occasioned considerable controversy in Catholic circles. Some Catholic missionaries who did leave felt his staying was a useless gesture—his presence could only bring harm to the Chinese clergy because he would be a continual reminder of opposition to the independent church. He would only stand in the way of any compromise with the government.

From then until 1960 there were two "glimpses" of Bishop Walsh. About two years after his house arrest, a member of the British diplomatic corps reported in Hong Kong that he had seen Walsh in Shanghai and that he was well. He was still under house arrest, living in the rectory of Christ the King Church with two Chinese priests who had joined the independent Catholic church. Walsh was giving no approval to the independent church, would not enter the church building, and said his Masses in his own room at the rectory.

The second "glimpse" came from a government announcement in September, 1955, that they would release twelve of the forty-one Americans held in prison in Shanghai. Nine were being released without further negotiation, but three had to ask for exit visas. Walsh was one of the three, but he never asked for a visa.

On March 17, 1960, the government announced that Bishop Walsh, together with Bishop Ignatius Kung Ping-mei and twelve Chinese priests, had been tried for treason and found guilty. He was sentenced to twenty years. He was sixty-nine. As with Wang Ming-tao's trial, nothing was said as to when and where the trial had been held, what the evidence was, or who had given it.

Earlier Bishop Walsh had written home:

I am a little tired of being pushed around because of my religion. My religion is all right; I don't see anything wrong with it. And that, come to think of it, is probably the world's prize understatement. Well, anyway, I don't feel inclined to get off the earth just because some people dislike my religion—or me because of it. I don't hold it against them, good souls; that's another matter. But what I say is, let them come and put me off. Is there anything wrong in that? I hope not. It seems merely normal and natural to me.[29]

Other Christian leaders of various denominations and groups were also imprisoned and arrested, especially after the celebrated "Hundred Flowers" period of 1956-57. This was the time when Mao Tse-tung felt secure enough to let everyone speak his mind freely—"Let a hundred flowers bloom, and a hundred schools of thought contend," was his way of opening the floor for debate. The invitation to freedom of expression was eagerly seized by church leaders as by other sections of Chinese opinion.

We have already quoted from Bishop Ting's speech attacking atheism (Chapter Six). Another remarkable attack was made by the Rev. Marcus Cheng, who was a vice-chairman of the Three-Self Patriotic Movement and a member of the Chinese People's Political Consultative Committee—the prominent evangelical president of the Chungking Theological Seminary who had been so fulsome in his reception of the Communists. He made a highly critical speech to the Chinese People's Political Consultative Committee which was reported in full both in the *People's Daily* (March 25, 1957) and in *Tien Feng* (May 13, 1957).[30] His subject was abuses of religious freedom. He began by quoting a recent speech of Y. T. Wu's:

No one disagreed with him [Wu] as he said, "Some churches have not been allowed to resume services, in some villages and small cities church buildings and furniture have been appropriated by various government organs, and the religious life of Christians has been interfered with. The policy has not been uniform, and some cadres have taken a hostile attitude throughout, forbidding subscribing money to the church, repairing church buildings or taking in new members. . . . Some cadres have not only not respected religious faith, but have even adopted an abusive attitude." Every one recognizes that these mistakes should be corrected.

. . . The contradiction between belief and unbelief, between theism and atheism, is a contradiction among the people, and not against an external element. We are all citizens of China, and this is not a contradiction between friends and enemies of the people, but an attempt at discrimination, at finding the truth. It is a contradiction of the "hundred schools."

Therefore believers have freedom to preach their faith, and unbelievers have freedom to criticize religion, and the attempt in this controversy to discover the truth should be carried out calmly, without abuse or name-calling. You speak out your atheism and I will preach my theism, and in this controversy you must not take to abusing my mother, defiling my ancestral graves or reviling my ancestors. In the eyes of us Christians, God is the Supreme Being, and the churches are His temples, the place where Christians worship Him. In the argument over theism and atheism you must not revile God, or blaspheme His name; you must not take our churches by force. . . . At the opening of a new steel bridge, an official of high rank . . . emphasized that this bridge had been made by human effort, and was not the work of any so-called God. Then he said, "You Christians should throw your God into the dungheap." Such blasphemy of God is, in the eyes of Christians, worse than reviling one's mother. This is not criticism, but abuse of religion. Chairman Mao in November 22, 1952, in a speech in Tibet said, "The Communist Party protects religion. Believers and unbelievers, believers in this or that religion, all are protected and respected." We believers appreciated very much this word from Chairman Mao, and what especially impressed and comforted us was his statement that the Government would not only protect, but would also "respect." Now this means that you must not blaspheme the God whom we worship, nor defile the churches in which we worship Him.

Cheng went on to say that Christians were prepared to forgive such abuse, and to differentiate between such mistakes and complete lack of freedom of religion. He also criticized the antireligious literature current in China.

It has been speculated that Marcus Cheng, conscience-smitten about what had happened to Wang Ming-tao and others, was making an attempt to atone for his past actions.[31]

For some time nothing happened to Cheng or to any of the others who criticized the government and the Party. But when the period of tolerance ended and the government clamped down on the "rightists" Marcus Cheng was among those denounced. However, he was able to keep his position of leadership.

The period of "grace" ended in November, 1957. An enlarged session of the Executive Committee of the Three-Self Movement was called by the government, which 130 Protestant representatives from all over the country attended. Y. T. Wu and eight other prominent leaders of the Three-Self Movement proceeded to denounce six "rightist" church leaders: Liu Ling-chiu, editor of the Christian magazine *The Farmer;* Chou Ching-tse, Amoy pastor; Tung Hung-en, Shanghai pastor; Fang Ai-shih, Ningpo pastor and chairman of a Methodist church there; Chou Fu-ching, Shanghai pastor; and Marcus Cheng.

Their crimes were that they had criticized the Communists in some way: the Communists had become corrupt in eight years whereas it took the Nationalists twenty-two; 80 percent of the farmers were dissatisfied with the new regime; Communist officals deceived the people with lies; the Three-Self Movement was very harmful to the religious life of the churches; there was true religious freedom in Hong Kong under British rule but not in China where Christians were mistreated and religion interfered with; Russia was wrong to put down the Hungarian revolution; the Chinese Communist Party should step down from the leadership of the country. Marcus Cheng's statements had been the most serious of all. His charges were "the greatest defamation ever made against the Communist Party, against the Constitution and the religious policy of the Government."[32]

These denunciations in Peking set the pattern for the delegates to follow against church leaders in their own localities throughout 1958. This was to be the year of great changes—the year of the "Communes" and the "Great Leap Forward." The combination of these two campaigns, concurrently with the campaign against "counterrevolutionaries" and "rightists" in the churches, and the demand for their greater subordination to the government-controlled Three-Self Movement, produced a radical change in Christian witness and church activities.

Church attendance declined rapidly. Peking, for instance, had sixty-five churches at the beginning of the year, and each had good attendance. By the middle of the year not more than 500 attended church in all of Peking. (Wang Ming-tao used to preach to 1000 or more each Sunday just in his church.) Whether as a result of poor attendance or as the next step in a carefully pre-planned campaign, the Communists' next move was to call for the unification of all churches. As we have already seen (Chapter Six), Peking's sixty-five were reduced to four, one in each section of the city. All the others were closed. Shanghai's two hundred churches were reduced to twenty-three. And so on throughout the country.[33]

The Three-Self Movement was responsible for all the details of unification under the Religious Affairs Bureau. The process involved surrender of all church property and control of church programs to the Three-Self Movement local Committee. Then the representatives of each denomination voted themselves out of existence.

How this was accomplished may be gathered from the typical example of Taiyuan, capital of Shansi Province. Taiyuan was a large city with churches belonging to the Church of Christ in China, Brethren, Assemblies of God, China Inland Mission, Seventh-Day Adventist, Salvation Army, and the indigenous Christian Assemblies. There was also a Taiyuan Y.M.C.A. These are the articles of union, as agreed upon by all these organizations:

There shall be unified worship, for the city of Taiyuan and a ministerial staff of three or four. All fellow-workers besides these and those assigned, to the Three-Self office, shall throw themselves into the Socialist construction of our mother country; those who are old or physically weak shall retire. All real and movable church property and all church funds shall be turned over to the Three-Self Patriotic Committee.

Church Organization

1. All former governing committees and boards of the various churches are hereby abolished and the administration of the church shall be in the hands of the Three-Self Patriotic Committee.
2. Regarding ritual, regulations and church order:
   a. There shall be a unified worship program and each church shall surrender its own individual ritual.
   b. The hymns used in worship shall be unified and a committee shall choose and edit the hymns for use.*

---

*This sample of a new political hymn is given in Lyall, *op. cit.,* p. 84:
    Thanks to the Communist Party and president Mao,
    For after Liberation the Church has been united;
    We are no longer divided into denominations;

   c. All books used in the interpretation of the Bible shall be examined and judged, and those containing poisonous thoughts shall be rejected. Only teachings favoring union and socialism shall be used. In particular any material coming from outside [China] shall be carefully examined before being accepted.

   d. There shall be no more preaching about the Last Day, or about the vanity of this world. This is negative and pessimistic teaching. Instead we shall emphasize the need for the union of faith and practice, the dignity of labor, the control of nature, and the dividing line between ourselves and our enemies, between right and wrong.

   e. Belief and unbelief shall not be made an issue in determining the marriage question.

3. In regard to the necessary reform of each church:

   a. The Little Flock shall abolish its women's meetings, its weekly breaking of bread, its personal interviews with members before the breaking of bread and its rule against women speaking in the church.

   b. The Salvation Army shall give up all its military regulations.

   c. The Seventh-day Adventists shall abolish their daily morning prayers. On the Sabbath day they shall participate in beneficial, good works and economic production. Their tithe system for the support of the clergy shall be abolished and also their unification of accounts for Shansi Province.

   d. All the YMCA Secretaries shall be assigned to productive labor, and the closing of the Taiyuan YMCA as a separate organization shall be carefully considered.[34]

On January 5, 1959, Y. T. Wu summed up the changes of 1958, the year of great changes, in these words:

We Christians during the past year have been deeply disciplined. Through socialist education the clergy and the laity of the whole country have had their thinking raised to a new level; the rightists have been

---

      We are no longer divided into those who have and
        those who have not;
      We have self-propagation, self-support and self-
        government;
      We are not now oppressed by imperialism;
      Our standard of living has been raised;
      We live in a society which is free and happy.

decisively defeated; the semi-colonial aspect of the Church has been changed; and the Chinese Church is now in the process of shaking off the shackles of imperialism and ready to advance on the road to socialism.[35]

And, later in the year, as part of the "Ten Year Celebrations," he expanded this to include:

The rumors spread by imperialists and reactionaries both before and after Liberation made many Christians afraid of the Communist Party, so that they doubted its religious policy. But ten years of experience have shown us that Christians, as well as believers in other religions, have complete liberty of religious belief; church activities such as Sunday worship, prayer meetings, Sunday School, baptism of new members, and ordination of pastors, and church agencies such as theological seminaries, the Bible House, and publishing houses all have proceeded as usual; religious belief is not only protected but also respected. These ten years have shown that the Party is not only determined to carry out its policy of freedom of religious liberty, but that its protection and concern for us are all-embracing. Christians have an entirely equal status among the people, on every level of the people's congresses Christians as well as believers in other religions are deputies. . . .

The past ten years have been glorious ones. The great accomplishments of these years have stirred not only the Chinese people, but all people throughout the world who love peace and have a hope in the future. Our Great Leap Forward, and our determination to continue to press forward, both demonstrate that our task is a righteous one, and that such a righteous task will not be hindered or perverted by any power whatever. . . .[36]

CHAPTER NINE

Christianity, 1968—and the Communist Dilemma

IN THE PRECEDING CHAPTERS there have been outlined the various developments affecting Christianity in Communist China between the years 1949 to 1962, at several levels and among differing groups. From a very confused situation the impression emerges of a struggling, then increasingly confident, church witness. Deprived of a formal structure and traditional practices, it has not only managed to survive but even, incredibly, to expand.

In 1967 the question that intrigued the outside observer of the Chinese scene was: "Is there a growing conflict in China between the militantly atheistic Communist authorities and what were supposed to be the routed forces of Christianity?" This appeared to be so from the reports reaching Hong Kong from many sources and, more important, from the increasing number of articles on religion in the leading Chinese secular newspapers and journals.

While there was little evidence that the Chinese Communist authorities had any reason to expect or fear a resurgence of revitalized Christianity after eighteen years of uneasy coexistence and adjustment, there was considerable evidence of a concern in Peking over the part that religion could play in the present widespread, second-generation weariness—to put it cautiously—with austerity, slogans, incessant meetings, Party meetings, and unproductive sacrifice.

The possible threat from religion in this present phase became apparent in 1963. Articles on the subject indicated that the Communist leaders were aware of a nationwide, unhealthy and even dangerous interest in the subject despite all the measures taken.

Since 1963 at least fifteen major articles and scores of lesser articles on religion have appeared, almost all of them in the widely circulated secular press, not the religious press. How the public debate began has been described by one of the leading protagonists, Ya Han-chang:

Between the years of 1959 and 1964 I had several articles about atheism published in the press. . . . Upon the publication of these articles Comrades Yu Hsiang and Liu Chun-wang also had three articles published at various times between 1963 and 1964, criticizing me on a number of points. Because their criticisms were erroneous I accordingly wrote some counter-criticisms. It was in this way that the debate over religion started.

It might well have been true that this particular "debate over religion started" in this way, but the reasons behind it went much deeper. Writing in the *Hong Kong Standard,* on March 12, 1962, its news editor, Jack Chow, an outstanding Christian and member of the Little Flock, said in a lead article:

To thousands upon thousands of Christian faithful—Catholics and Protestants—in Communist China the Old Testament passage, "God is our refuge and strength, a very present help in trouble" (Psalm 46:1) has become an increasingly empirical reality and a power to carry through.

Although the visible and formal churches are dying out on the mainland, *the invisible, formless, non-political and true ones are growing in numbers in Shanghai, Nanking, Peking and other towns and cities* [author's italics].

Jack Chow went on to say that the number of churchgoers had dropped considerably in recent years, due mainly to the fact that a great majority of the churches had been either closed or used by the Communist authorities as office buildings or local government offices. The churches that were still open were supported and controlled by the Communist government; and although church services were still held every Sunday, "Marxist-Leninist doctrine must be preached at the same time." The invisible churches, on the other hand, "or those devout believers who have left their respective churches voluntarily because they wanted no politics in their religion," had stood firm and had carried on their Christian activities privately and at tremendous risks.

Jack Chow gave an example: "One of the arrivals, the wife of a former professor at Peking University, belonged to a small prayer group of four Christian women prior to her departure from Shanghai. She says that there are many such small groups formed by people whose churches have either been shut down or taken over by the Communists. They meet irregularly but not infrequently at different homes for prayer-meetings, Bible study and fellowship. They have won many souls who have found God a great help in time of trouble. When they pray together they do not kneel and their meetings, which have no form of any sort, are usually short because they do not wish to invite trouble. The Communists forbid religious meetings at private homes. If more than two persons are found praying together at home, they are liable to prosecution on 'counter-revolutionary' charges and imprisonment."

Jack Chow then gave several examples of Christians who had been caught preaching or praying with small groups and who were given terms of imprisonment from two months to twelve years.

That this was not a biased report was evident from the statements made by pro-government sources inside China itself. A report at the Second Three-Self General Conference in January, 1961, had called for rooting out reactionary elements from the church which were carrying on "illegal activities in secret."[1] Four years later an editorial in *Tien Feng* (March 31, 1965), indicated that the Communist authorities were still far from happy about the state of Christian witness in China. The editorial observed that the national economy had developed rapidly in spite of national disasters, and that there was a "new spirit" everywhere as the people moved forward with complete faith in ultimate victory. But it was noted with some acerbity that Christians still had much to do: "Achievements in Christianity cannot compare with achievements in other fields. This shows that we are not doing enough." The editorial then posed the question: "What are our tasks as Christians in the present situation?" and proceeded to give a detailed five-point answer:

1. *To develop further Christian anti-imperialism.* In the last few years, the Christian Three-Self Patriotic Movement has made great achievements. Chinese Christianity has thrown off imperialistic control and basically has become a religion organized by the Chinese people themselves. However, the Christian anti-imperialist task is far from ended. *Imperialism has not suffered gladly its defeat in China, and is still plotting to return to power among the Chinese. . . . Although imperialists in religious garb were expelled from the China mainland, for more than ten years they have been banding together in Hong Kong and Taiwan, constantly making use of Christianity to carry on subversive activity against China. . . .* They dream of setting up a new anti-Communist crusade, using "unity," "witness," "service" and other such religious phrases to overthrow the Socialist countries. [Author's italics.]

2. *To develop studies of anti-imperialism, law-abiding patriotism, internationalism and Socialism . . .* in order to understand better the greatness and lovableness of our fatherland, the excellence of the Socialist system, the deep meaning of the three red banners of the General Line, the Great Leap Forward and the People's Communes, and the responsibility of the Chinese people in the struggle against Imperialism for world peace.

3. *To help further the government policy of freedom of religious belief.* Since liberation, the relevant departments of the government have everywhere put into practice the Party's policy of allowing freedom of religious belief. In the future, we should further help the government to put their policy into practice. This work can be divided into three parts: (1) to intensify study of the religious policy by pastors and laymen *so that everyone understands it completely;* (2) to continue to practice the principle of arranging religious activities with the primary aim of obeying the laws of the government—*religious activities should take place in church,* and should not interfere with production; (3) *to beware of admitting reactionary elements into the church* and of using Christianity for reactionary and subversive activities. We must help the government stop all illegal activities, using the cover of Christianity. [Author's italics.]

4. *To make strenuous self-reforms.* In the past few years pastors everywhere have persisted in political studies and have made good progress. . . . According to their varying capacities, fellow workers have also taken part in labor disciplines. Through these disciplines they have begun to change their understanding of labor and of the working people. . . . However, we must also admit that self-reform is a long process. . . . There will be many difficulties and many setbacks. Pastors and laymen should study political questions more earnestly and continue to labor according to their different capacities.

5. *To develop further Christian historical research.* The task of compiling historical materials has developed considerably in many Three-Self patriotic organizations. . . . Generally speaking, however, this work is still in the beginning stage, and it must be further developed. . . . By historical research we see more clearly the aggressive qualities of Imperialism and the political thought involved in self-reform.

Several important factors may be detected in this editorial. The predominant interest of the Three-Self Movement is "anti-imperialism," and not the salvation of souls or the spiritual upbuilding of the church. Every statement and activity of every member should have political significance, with continuing support for the government, and love for God and one's neighbor is not mentioned.

More important still, there are things that still need to be done or to be done better. After several years of study, education, and reform by labor disciplines, is it possible that even in the Three-Self Patriotic Movement there are still those whom the Communist officials suspect if not fear? For at least six years before this editorial, all religious activities had been held inside the church, according to strictly enforced laws, and yet item (2) under point 3 above indicates that religious meetings of considerable concern to the authorities were still being held outside the church and the authorities were unable for some reason to take direct action. As a result Three-Self Movement members were being threatened and warned.

And who are the "reactionary elements" whom the Three-Self Movement churches are to beware of admitting? With all the controls, organizational and personal, noted in previous chapters, are there links, tenuous but with far-reaching possibilities, between some of the anguished conformists of the Three-Self Patriotic Movement and the defiant purists of the indigenous "underground home congregations"? How else is one to interpret the statement "using

Christianity for reactionary and subversive activities" and "illegal activities using the cover of Christianity"?

For, although there are still some contacts kept with the traditional denominations outside China, both Catholic and Protestant, by and large these are considered too dangerous to be developed for their Chinese church members by the cautious and sympathetic representatives in Hong Kong, Taiwan and elsewhere. In writing this book I found it extremely difficult to get those with contacts in mainland China to talk about conditions there, for fear of causing hurt to Chinese friends.

The most likely explanation is that the proliferation of "underground home congregations" in mainland China, and the sympathetic association of the deeply compromised but nevertheless truly national government-controlled churches, has been paralleled to a remarkable extent by a similar movement among the twenty million overseas Chinese.

When Kuomintang party members fled to Hong Kong and Taiwan, particularly, there was a sudden increase in indigenous Chinese Christian activity. In Hong Kong there are four Christian Assemblies (Little Flock) with a membership of some two or three thousand. In Taiwan, in the mid-1950's, they increased to over forty thousand, several of the women being in Madame Chiang's Chinese Christian Women's Prayer Groups, of which there are over one thousand branch groups throughout Taiwan. The True Jesus Church also numbers over fifty thousand. These and several other smaller independent Chinese churches, deeply sympathetic and attached to their suffering fellow Christians on the mainland, are apparently at the root of what is troubling the Communist leaders in Peking. We shall return to this again later, but for the moment I would like to finish recording the evidence of Communist concern.

The debate on religion going on in the Communist press since 1963 has not been between Communists and Christians, but between Marxist theorists. Those taking part are all agreed that religion is a bad thing and ought to be got rid of; but the point at issue is how to do this after nineteen years of intense application of all kinds of measures while the Constitution allows people "freedom of belief"? The fact that, after nineteen years, Christianity—either in a nucleus of its organized Three-Self Movement form, or in its unorganized "underground home congregation" form—shows no signs of "withering away" but is even on the increase is at the root of the continuing official concern.

In his articles Ya Han-chang dealt with three categories—deist ideas, religion, and feudal superstitions—and he maintained that while these have much in common, "they are not the same thing." Ya Han-chang's critics on the ultra-Marxist side disagreed with this conclusion, insisting that all categories came under the same heading of religion. To support their theory, they quoted Engels' "scientific definition" of religion: "All religion is none other than an illusory reflection in the mind of man of the external forces that dominate him in his everyday life. In this reflection, human forces take the form of superhuman forces."

They supported their claim that the three categories are all one by pointing out that when religion is discussed in the classical works of Marxism-Leninism, no parallel mention is made of the deist idea and feudal superstitions; therefore the term "religion" must include them all. Ya Han-chang, however, maintained that the deist idea and feudal superstition were omitted because they were not relevant, since in the West religion was mainly Christianity, and feudal superstitions such as were found in China were practically unknown.[2]

The official definition had been laid down at the start of the debate in 1963:

Religion and superstition have their similarities. They also have their differences. All religious activities are superstitious activities. This is their similarity. But not all superstitious activities are religious activities. This is their difference.[3]

The reason why all true Communists had to be atheists and work for the elimination of religion and superstition was that one of the greatest dangers to socialism lay in religious belief:

Religious superstitious thoughts constitute a serious threat to socialist revolution and its construction. Socialist revolution aims to exchange the old social system of exploitation and oppression and to destroy classes. On the other hand, religion teaches people to seek happiness, solve the problems of life and reach the happiness of the after-life through prayer. Therefore, belief in religion must make revolutionary ardor fade.[4]

"Superstition," according to official Communist thinking in Peking, was divided into two distinct categories: "religious" superstition and superstitious activities, which were "neither the activities of any religion nor any religion in themselves."

"Religious superstition" was divided into two further categories originally used by Engels: "spontaneous religion," including ancestor worship; the worship of the lords of natural objects such as sun, earth, moon, wind, rain, water, and fire; and the worship of various other gods and ghosts; and "artificial religion," including Christianity, Buddhism, Islamism, Judaism, Hinduism, and Taoism. Superstition which was outside religion included exorcism to cure disease, fortune-telling, physiognomy, and geomancy.

The chief reason given for the official objection to the "artificial religions" was "because of their next life theory." According to the *People's Daily* (April 8, 1963) the "artificial religions" held that: "The afflicted, if they want to free themselves from suffering, must build up happiness for their 'next life' and must wait till after death for their souls to rise to the 'Kingdom of Heaven' (Paradise)."

This attitude, the Chinese Communists feared, would rob people of their desire to carry on the revolution. But their stock argument, after fifteen years of Communist government, was weak—that "religion is an instrument of exploiting classes used to convince man that he should meekly endure the oppression and exploitation of the exploiting classes." Who, in new China, constituted the "exploiting classes" advocating a "religion" which said a person "should meekly endure the oppression and exploitation"? All the evidence would seem to point to the fact that the "oppression and exploitation" came from the nonreligious Communist government officials.

The prominent intellectual, Feng Ting, who came under such vicious attack by the Communist regime in 1964, was accused of the crime of "bourgeois thought" and "subjective idealism" in his writings (especially in his book *Communist Way of Life,* which had a reported circulation of 860,000) for saying:

If happiness means living a normal life, that is living in peace without war, eating well, dressing beautifully, living in spacious and clean quarters, and having love and harmony between husband and wife and between parents and children, this is undoubtedly correct and it is what we all pray for.[5]

But he was wrong. This is not what true Chinese Communists

"pray for." In their view happiness goes hand in hand with revolution, and revolutionary ardor fades in a harmonious and peaceful environment. Therefore, religion—particularly Christianity, which purveys these truths and possibilities—must be eliminated from the Chinese scene.

In the words of *China Youth*: "Apart from class, apart from the collective, there is no revolution, no Communism, nor, naturally, any happiness."[6]

This was the "bourgeois" attitude of those in China who were now saying apparently: "Seeking comfort and ease is common human nature. I once dreamed of a summer house on the beach of a blue sea, surrounded by linden trees, with snow white sets of sofas and the best radios and televisions within and a small silver grey car outside. . . . Is not such a life the happiest?"

The answer is "no." The true "proletarian" attitude was really displayed by those who said: "Happiness means loyalty to the cause of mankind and the sacrifice of all things personal for the collective. . . . The standard of our happiness and misery is not material comfort or easy work but spiritual joy when serving the people."[7]

And all activities in mainland China in 1967 were influenced by the increasing necessity being forced on the aging revolutionaries in Peking of keeping the Communist revolutionary spirit alive. The recent and continuing "socialist education" campaign and the "intensify the class struggle" movement were both initiated to overcome the growing disinterest among second-generation Communists with strong tendencies to the "bourgeois" thinking described above. As one newspaper explained the task: "We must educate and influence the younger generation with proletarian thinking and socialist trends and splash bright red color on the pure souls of children."[8]

It is against this background that an evaluation of the official Communist attitude toward Christianity in China today must be made. If after nineteen years of stringent measures acted on in all the glow of revolution, Christianity has not only survived but has emerged with a nucleus of unshakable faithful, then the second-generation Chinese, tired of slogans and endless political meetings, might be won over in considerable numbers by dedicated lay Chinese Christians. The gospel which they have is their own gospel, not inherited from a Western-financed foreigner with Western-oriented ideas. The church which they form is a Chinese church with its own identity and character, forged in the fires of persecution before God and man, and no longer a pale, weak shadow. The vision which the members share is a real and living thing for the dangerous and difficult present and not just a pie-in-the-sky opiate. They are the truly free men and women in a country rapidly losing the excitement of promised new freedoms in empty slogans and bondage.

No wonder the Communist leaders were in a quandary. The one measure left to them was to drop the pretense of "freedom of religion" and openly launch a campaign to kill off all Christians. But they were aware that, while they might well survive the blow to their prestige, such a step would involve repercussions in their relations on the Asian and international scene. And making martyrs—especially of law-abiding Chinese nationals—was one sure way of giving fresh impetus to the Christian cause.

So, they concentrated on trying to make communism—the fiery, vision-filled communism of the long march and caves of Yenan—a more attractive alternative. The "gospel according to Mao" is being preached with Billy Graham-like fervor in nationwide crusades. The winners of the World Table Tennis championship were described as "bubbling with revolutionary zeal . . . particularly after studying and creatively applying Mao Tse-tung's thinking."[9] Sheng-yu, the shepherd, whose wife was breast-feeding her baby girl, persuaded her to lay the baby aside and feed a new-born lamb instead because "it is Chairman Mao who has enabled us to love the happy life we have today."[10] Chiang An-cheng, a trouble-making youngster, "showed a great change after he studied Chairman Mao's works," and "the masses commented, 'The skinny boy has become a good boy.' "[11] One group in Tingyuan Commune, Yuchung-hsien, Kansu Province, "has 141 families and a population of 842" who "studied Chairman Mao's works and underwent fundamental changes"; they are being used as a model pilot project for the whole nation to follow.[12] For "Mao" read "Christ"; for "change" read "conversion"; for "Party" read "church"; for "principles" read "doctrine"; for "rethinking" read "repentance"; for "happiness" read "peace"—and you have the evangelical Christian gospel.

But the very success of the campaign, it would seem, merely serves to breed disquiet in the minds of Communist leaders in Peking. For they reason, with sound logic, what is being done by high-pressured Communist campaigns could with equal or even greater success be undone by Christian preaching. It would need only a speech by some latter-day Chinese Luther or Savonarola to set the country ablaze— not with "counterrevolutionary activity," but with a defiant, unmanageable, and unpredictable Christian movement of protest. For the present, there is no evidence of this, but all the elements are there: the thousands of Christian converts reported from labor camps in West China, Sinkiang, Kansu, and Manchuria, as Christianity is spread among those who have no more left to lose; or the report of one of the highest Chinese officials in Tibet, a Christian, who was imprisoned because he insisted on praying and spreading his Christianity. (This was told me personally by Tsarong Shapé, "the Churchill of Tibet," just before he left India for Tibet and death in the Tibetan revolt of 1959. The Chinese official was billeted in his house in Lhasa and always prayed at meals and spoke of Christ. Tsarong Shapé said that he had to be released from prison because he was so essential in his official capacity, but he continued with his Christian witness.)

The rise of the "cultural revolution" in mid-1966, and the emergence of the fanatical Red Guards, brought open persecution of Christians. A front-page article in Hong Kong's leading English language newspaper,[13] written by its Shanghai correspondent, declared in 1966: "Christianity in Shanghai comes to an End" and continued:

The final page of the history of Christian religion in Shanghai was written on August 24.
On that day all the churches, active and inactive, whether conducted by their meager congregations or preserved by the Shanghai Municipal Bureau of Religious Cults, were stripped of the crosses, statues, icons, decorations and all church paraphernalia by the revolutionary students, wearing Red Guard armbands and determined to eradicate all traces of imperialist, colonial and feudal regimes.

The article listed some of the churches destroyed—the Zikawei Roman Catholic Cathedral, the Anglican Cathedral, Moore Memorial Church, and others. Then it continued:

Books used in services, religious tracts and archives found in the churches were burnt in bonfires in front of the churches. On Yuen Ming Yuen Road, where several missionary societies formerly had their offices and store rooms, the literature was burnt on the road in front of the offices.

Another article in the same newspaper, published on Christmas Day, 1966, reported:

No Christmas services are being held this year in Peking's churches, closed last August at the height of the Red Guards' campaign to enforce the tenets of China's great "proletarian cultural revolution."
It is thought to be the first time this century that Peking's Christians —now estimated to number fewer than 20,000 out of more than six million people in the capital—are not holding public Christmas worship.
The constitution of the Chinese People's Republic upholds the right of religious worship, and in recent years, Christmas has been marked by midnight masses and special services in the two Roman Catholic cathedrals, one convent and one small Protestant church.
In August, the Red Guards closed and partially desecrated the capital's churches, and foreign nuns were expelled from China.

"One with God is a majority," said St. Theresa. As the Chinese Christians increase in their confidence of faith, they draw nearer to the situation of the agonizing Job, who, with nothing left but his filth and boils, could cry: "He [God] shall break in pieces mighty men without number, and set others in their stead. Therefore he knoweth their works, and he overturneth them in the night, so that they are destroyed. . . . When he giveth quietness who then can make trouble? and when he hideth his face, who then can behold him? Whether it be done against a nation, or against a man only" (Job 34:24-29).

The time, and the man for the time, may be very near. Watchman Nee, founder of the Little Flock, sentenced to fifteen years' imprisonment in 1952-53, was due out of prison in 1968. Unlike Wang Mingtao, he has never signed a confession and, although reputedly ill on one or two occasions, he is still sound of mind. For the past few years it is said that he has been working on translations of technical books while in prison and has greatly impressed the Communist officials with his erudition and ability.

The many thousands of Little Flock members in Hong Kong and Taiwan are able to keep in touch with the situation inside China through relatives, friends, and business colleagues. It is reported among them that the Communists are in a considerable dilemma. They would like to retain Watchman Nee for his technical ability as a research scientist and also to avoid the adverse publicity of his leaving China and becoming a major figure in the influential Little Flock circles among overseas Chinese. Also, since his imprisonment several books of addresses which he had given have been published in English (for example, *The Normal Christian Life, The Normal Church Life, What Shall This Man Do?, Concerning Our Missions, Sit, Walk, Stand, The Release of the Spirit*) which have been well received in Christian circles in the West, especially America.

But, like Wang Ming-tao, he is a representative figure to tens, if not hundreds, of thousands of Chinese Christians; and like Wang Ming-tao, he would not be prepared to accept enforced silence. A man with a deep sense of the Christian's individual and corporate responsibility to the fellow-workers of the Church of Christ, a scholar and gifted expositor, an attractive personality and leader of great ability, his sixteen years of imprisonment and considerable gifts would ensure him a tremendous following.

Even if he leaves China the problem remains. As has been noted already, the Little Flock now has Christian Assemblies throughout Southeast Asia with over forty thousand members in Taiwan alone. For the past ten years they have tended more and more to isolate themselves in a form of exclusivism similar to that of the "Exclusive Brethren" of the West, through the teaching of a former colleague of Watchman Nee, Witness Lee. But recently there has been a strong reaction against this trend, and several of the younger members have been demanding a return to the open principles set out by Watchman Nee's exposition of the New Testament.

Naturally, most of this is carried into mainland China in conversations and letters, and many Chinese Christians living outside China would like Watchman Nee to come out and join them in the great task of carrying a revitalized Christianity to Asia and the West. At the same time, if he should choose to stay inside China, the momentum and significance of such a movement would not leave him or others untouched and would have far-reaching possibilities for Christian witness in China.

Just as inside China the trend is to "underground home congregations," so in Taiwan, Hong Kong, Malaysia, Japan, the Philippines, and across Southeast Asia to India there is developing a new trend in

Christian witness—a return to the old, informal, apostolic, or New Testament "household church."

In a generation when the "wind of change" is blowing strongly, sweeping away political traditions in the newly independent countries of Asia and Africa and Latin America, a Christianity that was becoming weak and tradition-hardened is being forced by the inevitable pressures of history in general and communism in particular to rethink its principles and readjust its practices in order to survive.

It is not beyond possibility that the instrument that is being forged in China, and among the Chinese Christians scattered abroad, in the hot fires of persecution may yet be the weapon in the hand of God to smite the Philistines and Pharisees of the twentieth century.

One of the most recent and illuminating articles to come out of Communist China is yet another from the verbose duo, Yu Hsiang and Liu Chun-wang, in continuation of their "great debate."[14] Summarizing Ya Han-chang's theories in previous articles they state:

Comrade Ya Han-chang denies that religion is an ideology. His opinion is that a religion must have tenets, church rules and professional religionists. It must be something having organized public bodies to carry out its activities. . . . In his opinion, the struggle to speed up the extinction of religion is aimed at the extinction not of religious ideas in the people's minds but of "religious organizations, public bodies and activities." In his opinion, when religions with "organizations, public bodies and activities" have died out, then—regardless of how many people still believe in the soul, in ghosts, in spirits and in God—it will be time to proclaim the extinction of religion, will it not? Hence there will be no more task to fight against religion, will there?

Therefore, while the outlook is bleak for organized Christianity in Communist China, it would appear that there is considerable hope for its survival in the proliferating "underground home congregations"—ironically, self-supporting, self-governing, and self-propagating, but with small "s." This is my own conclusion, but it receives unexpected support from the nonreligious former Communist official Hsiao Feng, when he says: "During the land reform movement all the Catholic and Protestant churches in the villages and towns were closed, but 'underground home congregations' still existed. I wonder if it is not possible that in the future the 'home congregation' will be the most developed style of religious life."

At a time when countries throughout the world are becoming more and more isolated and nationalistic, I wonder if it is not possible that this may be Christian China's great contribution of the twentieth century.

I close this chapter with the significant and challenging words of the most Communist of the professing Christians in China, Y. T. Wu, taken from an article on the future of religion in China:[15]

My answer, in essence, is this: Let the Christian faith prove itself. If it is such a fragile thing that it cannot stand up in a critical philosophical environment, its death should be a matter of regret to nobody. But if it is the staunch, virile, life-giving faith that every devout Christian believes it to be, its vital testimony will always convince people because it meets the spiritual needs and eternal yearnings of the human heart. Indeed, a critical environment may help to search out those who profess the faith in name only—the seeds, in the words of Christ's parable, that fall by the wayside or on stony ground.

Late News of Watchman Nee

From a recent Asian News Report quoted in the February 1969 issue of *World Vision* magazine comes the word that Watchman Nee has not been fully released by the Communist authorities, although his sentence ended in April 1967. Nee is now in a Shanghai prison and is allowed home once or twice a month, but he may not stay overnight. He is still translating technical books into Chinese and receives a small salary for this work.

CHAPTER TEN

A Possible Future Strategy

ENOUGH EVIDENCE has been given in the preceding chapters to show that Christianity—a dynamic, expanding Christianity—has a future in China, whether the present extremist Communist regime remains in power or is replaced by a more moderate one.

If the Soviet Union may be taken as an example, together with the evident concern of the aging Chinese old-school revolutionaries at the lack of fervor in today's second-generation Communist youth, it is a reasonable deduction that within the next ten to twenty years there will be a more tolerant regime in Peking, certainly in matters of internal and external politics and economics, if not in religion. The twin issues of "revisionism" and "economism" which have been the basic factors in the convulsions of the 1966-68 "cultural revolution" are already being resolved by compromise. Right at the height of the monumental ideological controversy, with its nation-wide repercussions spilling over into neighboring Asian territories, the Peking authorities continued sending supplies of food to Hong

Kong, turned on the critical water supply to the British Colony on the agreed date and threw the whole weight of the Communist Party and Liberation Army machines into restoring peace in Kwantung Province in order that the prestigious Canton Fair be held more or less as usual.

These are only straws in the winds raging across the racked nation of China. Taken together with the repeated public declarations of leaders such as Chou En-lai that the country's economy must be restored, they have caused political observers to say that once some semblance of order has been obtained, the major emphasis will be placed on the restoring of normal trade relations with other countries. It has been conservatively estimated that the first eighteen months of the cultural revolution cost China $40,000,000 (U.S.) in direct trade with Hong Kong—and that does not take into consideration the inestimable damage done to her own economy.

China's desperate need, therefore, for foreign currency in the next few years may well be expressed in greater liberalizing of trading opportunities and providing even more attractive facilities for tourists to visit and spend money in China. This, in the next ten years, is the most that serious students of China are prepared to go on record as expecting.

What is not considered possible by any stretch of the imagination —except by uninformed "old-school" missionaries—is the reinstatement of Chiang Kai-shek, with the concomitant return of Western-style denominationalism. All serious Christian thinking about China should accept this as final. Western missionary paternalism is as dead as medieval feudalism. The antiquated reasoning and unrealistic hopes of missionaries in Taiwan and Hong Kong that the clock can be turned back thirty—and even more!—years to permit them a sentimental return journey have even less foundation than the futile and understandable expectations of the aging Chiang Kai-shek. For even in the unlikely event of his return to the mainland, and even if he then threw open the door to Western denominations and missions once more, those who took advantage of such a hypothetical opportunity would find themselves faced by a type of people and circumstances they were totally unprepared to reach. This is not to take into consideration, either, the incalculable damage to Christianity.

Having accepted with complete finality, then, the utter inadequacy of previous methods, the question arises: Is there any new strategy

whereby Christians in the West can help Christians in the East—in
this instance, in China—in their mutual responsibility of extending
the Kingdom of God in their generation of atheistic dialectical ma-
terialists? I think there is.

But, first of all, I would like to digress in order to outline a background against which to project a possible strategy. Christianity is
not making a great impact upon the vast numbers who inhabit the
Asian countries, and the cause may be traced as much to the influence of the West on Asia as to the basic resistance of Asians as
Asians to the gospel of Jesus Christ.

In the first place, the West has persistently regarded Asia as a
unity, often in the face of contradictory evidence, and this factor
alone has propelled the Asian countries to seek their own collective
identity *vis à vis* the West. It was once remarked of India's late
President Nehru that his anti-American streak was simply the British
side of him. And it would be more than a half truth to say that his
pan-Asian feelings were a product of his British education rather
than of his actual experience. Today Asians look for common
ground with other Asians, and the Western view of Asia is fed back
to the West by interested parties in China, Japan, India, Taiwan, the
Philippines and other Western-oriented Eastern countries.

There has also been a nationalist aftermath, centered in an attempt to keep pan-Asianism alive in order to deal with outside
powers. The fact of the cold war has brought tensions into Asia
that it might have escaped but for Western fears. And most countries have passed through successive phases of pro-Western, pro-
Communist, or neutralist attitudes before gradually rejecting all of
these attitudes for balanced considerations of national interest.

In such a climate Christianity has suffered.

As we have seen, Christianity in Asia, compared with the an-
tiquity of the Eastern cultures, is very much a newcomer. And relative to the population Christians are few. South India apart,
Christianity in Asia is usually not more than 150 years old, and may
be much younger. Except in the Philippines, in the most Christian
parts of South India, in parts of Indonesia and in Korea, Christians
of all sorts are normally a tiny fraction of the population. They are
seldom more than 5 percent and often less than 1 percent.

Thus, by any acceptable standard of definition it can reasonably
be conceded that Christianity has either failed as a movement or else

has never even really begun to have a significant impact on the culture. Dr. K. M. Panikkar, the Indian scholar-diplomat, speaks of what he calls the "Vasco da Gama epoch" of Asian history. Panikkar notes that Christianity in Asia shared with certain other aspects of Western culture the stigma of association with the imperialist expansion of the West during this era. And he concludes that the Christian mission in Asia has "definitely failed."

Nor is Panikkar alone in this judgment. It is widely held by many Asian intellectuals and by many churchmen, even in the West. Gabriel Herbert, for instance, made considerable use of Panikkar's work in his analysis of missionary weaknesses, although without adopting his conclusions.

But the evidence does not point to the failure of Christianity in and of itself; it points to the failure of the vehicle by which it was communicated. If Christianity has been rejected by Asians along with Westernism, the fact only supports Kenneth Scott Latourette's contention that the Church is never successfully planted in a culture previously alien unless there is also a profound and extensive communication between the Christian culture from which the missionaries came and the alien culture to which they go. Such a communication has been largely lacking in many Asian countries.

Significantly enough, some confirmation of this analysis is to be found in the writings of Asian Christians in recent years, in which the necessity of some form of dialogue with the great Asian religions has formed a persistent theme. Many argue that the need for dialogue has become more imperative as these religions have become more militant and their extreme right wings demand the expulsion of Western missionaries and the removal of Western cultural and financial influence.

A significant key to the success of Christianity in this encounter is the depth and extent of the witness of the dynamic gospel presented by the indigenous groups in several countries. Instinctively, these Christian groups with their simple New Testament approach to principles and practices have fastened on the crux of the approaching religious confrontation—the incarnation of the Son of God.

This "scandal of particularity," as it has been termed, is the greatest obstacle to the acceptance of Christ by Asians. In the past Asian intellectuals were able to reject the "scandal" because of its associations with "Western notions of superiority" in the various Western denominational missions; now, however, they are being presented with Christ by Asian nationals in Asian terms.

In the days when churches were wholly dependent on Western missions, theology (in the sense of a statement of God's dealings with men in the acceptable thought-forms of that particular time and in the context of that generation's beliefs, problems and heresies) was almost totally laid down by missionaries and accepted by nationals. Today, an increasing number of Asian Christians are realizing that they are responsible both for the purity of the Church's faith and the intelligibility with which it communicates that faith. Out of this double concern is being born a true theology, a theology which is not just an empty imitation of Western formulations but an attempt to express the whole counsel of God in terms that their fellow countrymen can make their own.

The excitement, the spiritual enthusiasm being generated by those Asians who are experiencing the outworking of the Scriptures in their everyday living, from peasants through professors to politicians, has to be felt to be believed. All around them the great Asian religions are becoming increasingly anachronistic in the twentieth century. And where these religions are attempting adjustment it is in secular terms in a dubious participation in national politics.

Apostolic Christianity, which is not *primarily* a religion for men to practice, but a message from the living God embodied in the incarnated, crucified and resurrected Christ, is relevant, practicable, and above all, "Asian." Sermons, worship, hymns, church gatherings, discipline and outreach—all are now being interpreted in Asian terms in several countries, from totalitarian China to democratic India. And this means, as theological dialogue increases in the next few years, that we may yet see the most significant expansion of Christian witness in Asia since the first centuries of apostolic teaching—and also perhaps a significant contribution to Western Christendom, increasingly baffled and frustrated by rigid denominational traditions.

What is imperative, therefore, is that serious and urgent thought should be given to combining the increasing Western concern over theoretical "lay" participation in church activities[1] and the developing Eastern pragmatism of individual and group self-sufficiency without historical additions and traditions. Instead of the present haphazard proliferation of similar but powerful unrelated movements, the present sectarian, pastor-missionary-centered church structure should begin moving at all levels of church practice to a more centripetal emphasis. Instead of congregations or groups helping the pastor or missionary, the latter should be helping the former to a more representative witness. Activities should move away more and more from the church building to the home—home Sunday schools, home Bible classes, "cottage meetings," neighbor-visiting. Teaching responsibility for the "layman" should not be confined to an occasional participation but should be developed and encouraged to cover every kind of group in possible future household gatherings. "Feed the flock of God which is among you" should be the responsibility of street and neighborhood elders, pastors and teachers in homes, instead of being limited to a few people in any kind of church building serving a whole district. In this way, whoever hears the good news of God in Jesus Christ, whatever kind of government may be in power, however antagonistic the opposition and whatever class or type of people are involved—a true Christian witness will survive and grow.

The first stage in any new strategy of missions, therefore, would be to collate the growing body of significant Asian conviction and witness, and harness it to an acceptable form of distribution. Thus we arrive, inevitably, at the problem of communication, the most significant problem of the twentieth century.

Mankind is today on the brink of a "communications revolution" that will change the patterns of life as profoundly as did the Industrial Revolution of the nineteenth century or the Agricultural Revolution of an even earlier period. What this means in terms of the expansion of the Christian gospel cannot be overestimated.

The Industrial Revolution of the nineteenth century provided the sinews—industries, capital, transport, etc.—which gave impetus to the next century's worldwide missionary expansion. Missionary societies in their "modern" form can be traced back to Wilberforce's "Clapham Sect," a voluntary society formed of his friends to produce reforms in Parliament (including the abolition of slavery) by gaining the support of the public. The rapid development of capitalism through an expanding industrialization and a growing social consciousness led to the formation of more and more philanthropic societies on the same voluntary pattern: businessmen

giving more and more of their time and ability, forming themselves
into groups on the pattern of a capitalist company in order to bring
their "spiritual ideas"—as opposed to Wilberforce's "social ideas"—
before the public, and soliciting support for their particular religious
cause. Support gained in this way would enable another missionary
to be sent out to whatever field particularly interested the "Board
of Directors."

The later "faith missions" were formed on the same religio-
capitalist "Board" system, whose function it was to promote and
propagate the ideas and works of their particular group associates.
The relative success of this system was assured by the overall
"umbrella" of the great imperialisms then existing. With the collapse
of imperialism between the two World Wars of the twentieth century
it was inevitable that the missionary strategy which was dependent
on it should collapse also.

Any new strategy, therefore, for the second half of the twentieth
century must take into consideration the new forces with which we
are surrounded—technology, nationalism, socialism, communications
—and the kind of vehicle which they will provide to communicate
the counsel of God.

On December 16, 1958, when an Atlas rocket was launched into
the sky from Cape Kennedy, Florida, the communications revolution began. This was Project Score, a rocket carrying a tape-recorder
which broadcast back to earth a Christmas message from President
Eisenhower.

Although Score was intended primarily to demonstrate the early
capabilities of space communications, it became an historic event;
a human voice, for the first time, had spoken from outer space via
a communications satellite.

The next six years brought a swift series of experimental communications satellites—the Echoes, the Telstars, the Relay, the
Syncoms—leading to the successful launching on April 6, 1965,
of Early Bird, the world's first commercial communications satellite.
Thus, Early Bird became the forerunner of a series of commercial
satellites that will constitute a worldwide system being developed
by the International Telecommunications Satellite Consortium
(INTELSAT), a partnership of over sixty countries formed as an
outgrowth of the Communications Satellite Act, passed by the United
States in 1962. These countries jointly own the satellites in the sys-

tem and individually own the earth stations. The Communications Satellite Corporation (COMSAT) acts as the manager for the Consortium and represents the United States of America in INTELSAT.

Today, Early Bird has two new, bigger and more powerful partners in the sky—one over the Atlantic Ocean and another over the Pacific—making it possible for people on opposite sides of the world to see and hear each other. Throughout 1968-69 a series of even larger satellites are being launched to provide coverage for all parts of the world.

Satellites, unlike other international modes of communications, are capable of transmitting all forms of communications simultaneously—telephone, television, radio, data and facsimile. No other means of communications transmission can do this over long distance at comparable low cost.

Furthermore, modern satellites are capable of transmitting all forms of communications *directly* between all earth stations within their lines of sight. Thus countries with low-cost earth stations can communicate with each other at the same time, in pairs, or in groups.

When stations are built in Latin America, for example, these countries will direct lines to Spain. Similarly, when stations are constructed in Africa, they will have direct lines to any country in Europe, North America or Latin America, and also within their own continental areas.

The unique capabilities of communications satellites are opening up new communications uses that were not practical until now because of the limitations of conventional means of transmission. Intercontinental television transmission is becoming accepted as routine. Since there are almost as many television sets in the world as there are telephones, television by satellite will have a profound impact on world news coverage, education, entertainment, and religious beliefs.

Closed circuit television can be extended by satellite for long distance transmission and therefore holds great educational potential. It may well revolutionize teaching methods in both the developed and developing countries. While many people in the less developed nations may not be able to read and write, they can see and hear. Thus they could be given a rudimentary training in health, agriculture, vocational and other skills, thereby lifting world standards.

Interim newspapers are already being transmitted over shorter distances via facsimile in Japan, Sweden, the United States and other countries. Satellites will expand this method of publication, because to a satellite distance has no meaning. Satellites will also change the patterns of international news operations. New York, London and Paris, traditionally the communications and news distribution centers of the world, will soon be joined by other cities.

At a minimum, satellites will speed and simplify the transmission of stories from remote areas. They will make it easier for the news services to distribute news in all forms, and will improve the ability of local media to better serve the growing interest of people in smaller towns in world events.

Computers on one continent have already corresponded with computers on another continent at speeds as much as fifty times faster than possible prior to the introduction of satellite communications. Thus it will be possible for the libraries of major countries to be available to scientists and scholars in other countries; for businesses with offices around the world to maintain up-to-date inventory control, and to control the quality and volume of production at plants in different countries from a central source.

This is only a preview of the future of satellite communications. Some are potentials; many are realities that are now, or soon will be, made available to all countries of the world. Over the next decade there will be established a worldwide communications system by which government, industries, or individual businessmen can establish contact with anyone, anywhere, at any time—by voice, sight, or document. When this occurs, the individual's ability to communicate will have transcended every barrier of time and space.

The development of these communications tools is far beyond the theoretical stage. Ultimately a master communications system will emerge that will utilize all of them. David Sarnoff, Chairman of the Radio Corporation of America and guiding genius in this field for the past sixty years, has said that it should be relatively easy to design and produce low-cost, single-channel television receivers for use in primitive or underdeveloped areas of the world. These sets could be built by assembly line techniques, housed in simple plastic or metal containers, and equipped with transistorized circuits consuming very little energy. They could be made to run on batteries, rechargeable by wind, hydraulic or even animal power. Such sets could be distributed throughout the developing regions in quantities suitable to local conditions. If they were programmed from regional stations transmitting through a few broadcasting satellites, the tragic effects of illiteracy could be virtually abolished in ten years. This application of broadcast satellites will represent a major achievement of the communications revolution.

A miniature "village" radio station is already being marketed in Australia which has a broadcasting range of 300 to 700 square miles, and is being sold at only $5,000 (U.S.) The station is built to international standards and is estimated to have a life of at least ten years before requiring major attention. The station can be installed by someone who has never seen a radio station before, and it comes with a "do-it-yourself" kit including instructions for both installation and operation. It includes a program mixer and console, with power from a small generator, and if a module (a drawer-like device carrying a printed circuit) failed, it could be pulled out, another inserted, and the failed one returned for repair. There are two microphones, a turntable and a tape-recorder to enable the operator to tape telephone calls or programs from larger transmitters.

These miniature radio stations are ideal for village communities and in the fast-developing newly emerging nations of Asia—and elsewhere—their potential is enormous. The 130-watt or 250-watt sizes take up no more space than a corner of a normal-sized room or hut, and the unit stands only 5 feet 6 inches high and depth is less than a foot.

Other developments now under way will also lead to a basic transformation of the entire communications structure. In London, at the end of 1966, a committee representing newspapers and news agencies in nearly every country in the world decided to prepare a scheme for using satellites to speed the flow of international news. It was suggested that in due course such a scheme could lead to the establishment of a world newspaper, published not necessarily by a commercial undertaking but by an international body.

In Asia in the spring of 1967, the Philippines and Thailand launched themselves into the satellite communications field by activating temporary ground stations for sending and receiving messages to and from the United States, Hawaii and Japan through the medium of a telecommunications satellite that has been orbiting over the Pacific Ocean since the end of 1966.

By the end of 1968 both of these countries will have completed permanent ground stations that will enable them to use satellites more extensively for communication with other countries. By that time, Hong Kong, Taiwan, Indonesia, Malaysia, Australia, and possibly other countries around the Pacific basin will have begun construction of ground stations, aiming at completion dates by late 1968 or early 1969.

The new members of the COMSAT system will be using the "Lani Bird," a telecommunications satellite, along with the United States and Japan who are already using it.

Hong Kong will have space-age contact with other countries when a giant dish-shaped scanner is completed in 1968. Ninety feet in diameter, the scanner will be the "eye" for a $5,000,000 (U.S.) earth satellite station. The station will be Hong Kong's link in a global satellite communications system operating by the end of 1968.

In 1969 three big satellites will be in fixed orbits—one over the Pacific, one over the Atlantic, and the third over the Indian Ocean. These three satellites will give full global communications coverage, and enable Hong Kong to "see" into the United States and "look" into Britain. They will also give Hong Kong a future television, telegraphic and telephone contact with other parts of the world—at least, with the fifty countries who have present use of the satellite communications.

Direct communication links with European capitals will be possible through the Indian Ocean satellite for India, Pakistan, Burma, and Ceylon who at present are unable to use the "Lani Bird."

A satellite communications ground station is the latest in national status symbols. Like oil refineries, national flag carrier airlines, or steel mills, they put a shine on the modern look of the developing country and have the kind of effect on the morale that status symbols often generate. However, the Asian governments have gone into this new field primarily because of the potential benefits and profit which they promise. Those who have been irked by their continuing dependence on communications facilities and channels owned by foreign cartels see in the new arrangement offered by satellite communication an opportunity to exercise control at least over the facilities within their borders.

The lower cost of international communications afforded by the use of satellites is also an important factor. The existing "Early

Bird" type of satellite costs about $10,000,000 (U.S.) to build and launch, and has a life expectancy of about five years. Split among a number of countries this initial cost is not a problem. The fact that it requires no maintenance also is extremely attractive.

The fact that sixty-two countries have already joined the "satellite club," and the readiness of international banks to make loans for financing ground stations at an average of more than $5,000,000 (U.S.) each, are indications of profit possibilities.

It is expected that each of the ground stations in Asia will have 240 channels. These can be used for radio-telephone, telex, facsimile transmission and the relay of radio and television programs. Once the permanent ground stations begin operating, the new Communications Revolution will have reached Asia.

I have gone into considerable detail in outlining the significance and structure of communications in Asia in order to demonstrate the mechanics of the second stage of a possible new strategy of missions—by using the technological, economic, political and social forces of the 1960's. Having outlined the system, however, is not to have solved the problems of utilizing the new communications revolution, which I see as similar to the old Industrial Revolution— the problems of men and money.

The key professional requirements of the "social-conscious" missionary movement arising out of the Industrial Revolution were economics, medicine and education. The *economics* consisted in the accumulation and use of great new sources of personal and corporate wealth arising out of the rapidly proliferating variety of industries. *Medicine* involved the increasing concern over the multiplicity of new diseases and new discoveries of medicines and surgical techniques. *Education* involved the newly released and relentless demand for a reservoir of informed and skilled people, both male and female, to fill the vast new fields opening up. The most obvious next step at the time for the concerned Christian was to export these benefits—and the nineteenth-century missionary movement was on its way. The other essential requirements were "spiritual" rather than "professional"—apostles, prophets, teachers, evangelists, etc.— requirements which are not influenced by historical changes. The money needed to finance their work was either direct, by open soliciting, or indirect, by voluntary subscription, as befitted their philanthropic-religio-capitalist character in an era when money was plentiful, consciences were sensitive and cost of living was low.

The key professional requirements for a new strategy arising out of the Communications Revolution are high finance, mass media and the humanities. *High finance* is a specialized branch of economics expertise and must be relieved of the nineteenth-century guilt feelings of owning earned or inherited wealth and devoted to the accumulating, organizing and administrating of the vast sums of money required for the new vehicles of communication—satellites, computers, publishing, press, radio and television facilities, etc. In the *mass media* one must acquire professional writing expertise in all aspects of communications—books, magazines, newspapers, radio and television presentation—and professional technical expertise in the operating and creative use of the rapidly developing mechanical facilities. *The humanities* are not to be limited to the study and practice of philology and polite literature; the term must be used in the wider and generic sense of the study of that group of interests relating to the whole field of human nature—philology, anthropology, theology, sociology, psychology, etc.

Just as in the early stages of the Industrial Revolution there were Christian leaders of vision and skill who placed an ineradicable imprint on their generation and century, so in the Communications Revolution there are men already highly placed in these fields who are deeply convinced Christians. But unlike their earlier counterparts, their vision and skills are not being realized or utilized to spread the Christian message but are being dissipated in vaguely unsatisfactory professional or academic pursuits as ends in themselves.

Three important steps are needed to harness and revitalize the men and their skills and to make them relevant at this particular time:

1. The recognition that the present international political climate will no longer tolerate any attempts to improve social and spiritual conditions in developing countries by political decisions made in the West—as for instance Wilberforce and slavery. The emergence of post-Second World War nationalisms, the United Nations and Western nations' aid projects, have combined to make the old systems and interests obsolete and to create the means and necessity for new vehicles of communications and help between countries.

The Chinese Communist authorities have succeeded to a remarkable degree in integrating all oral, informal, casual and traditional means of communication with the more conventional channels and methods of propaganda. Consequently, the present government in China has succeeded in bringing more people into direct and close contact with the central government than ever before in Chinese history.

A more acceptable form to Christians, however, would be a system which was not united to any government but was a privately organized and supported body such as is operated in South Korea. There a Communications Center combines all mass media facilities in one unit in order to inform and educate the people of that country along certain lines.

2. A decision to reject the concept and support of nineteenth-century type missions, and consequent withdrawal of all finance and personnel from such activities, and to accept the concept of the Church of Jesus Christ as a living organism capable of implantation and expansion in any country irrespective of political, social and religious bias.

3. The founding of regional Christian Communications Centers, staffed by Christian professionals from a variety of disciplines—e.g. anthropologists, sociologists, political scientists, and others, as mentioned earlier—as well as the writers and technologists of all communications mass media, whose chief aim and function would be the development and expansion of these living churches in every form of society in any country—from the primitive tribal to the sophisticated urban. These Christian Communications Centers would be financed by like-minded churches, wealthy individuals, institutions and foundations contributing in the first instance to a Christian Communications Fund, advised and administered by a body of Christian businessmen expert in the intricacies of high finance. The Centers could be either financially viable after a given period by means of returns on capital investment, or supported, depending on local circumstances.

In the initial stages five of these Communications Centers could be set up—one in the United States, one in Asia, one in South America, one in Europe, and one in Africa—in order to provide a basic worldwide link-up. Later, subsidiary units in the different areas could be developed from the parent Center. Within five years these Centers could be producing a body of the most highly trained professional experts in communications media to be found anywhere in the world—and forged out of a living spiritual unity of all that is vital in a universal gospel. They would be able to hold down the key jobs in their own countries (e.g. Hong Kong would take students from all surrounding Asian countries until each had a unit of its own) in this most significant phase of communications development in the next decade, and through these most important positions influence their fellow countrymen with their own informed and dynamic Christianity.

These Christian Communications Centers would contain:

(1) A research unit, responsible for investigating cultural patterns, national and tribal mores, political systems, linguistics, individual and organizational problems, parapsychological phenomena, mass persuasion techniques and how to combat them, etc.

(2) Computers, to collate all information gathered.

(3) Library, for above.

(4) School of Journalism, with Christian professionals teaching and supplying.

(5) Press, radio and television facilities and materials.

(6) International News Agency Bureau, to supply Christian interpretation of all news gathered from trained sources.

(7) Publication Unit to print and publish books, magazines and newspapers.

But, you might ask at this stage, *how can all this be used to help the cause of Christ in China?*

In this way. Such a Communications Center in Hong Kong, linked to other countries in other continents and serving all the countries of Asia, would naturally have its greatest impact on China. Chinese Christian students would almost certainly be in the majority, whether taken from Hong Kong, Taiwan or from among the twenty million other overseas Chinese.

This is already more than a vision for the future. A gifted Chinese Christian, Timothy Yu, a graduate in communications and editor for more than twenty years, is already laying the foundation for such a Center. He has already established a commercially viable publishing house, has founded a school of journalism sponsored by the Hong Kong Baptist College, is organizing an Asian Christian

Writers' Conference, and is planning for a full Christian Communications Center to be opened in Hong Kong in 1971 with the support of Chinese and Western businessmen and professionals.

With Hong Kong linked to the worldwide satellite system these highly trained and enthusiastic Chinese Christian journalists/researchers/technologists will be able to collect the most up-to-date information on their own countries, on other countries and on the work of God, and use it in newspaper and magazine articles, radio and television broadcasts beamed *direct* into China for the encouragement and expansion of the Church there.

The Church of Jesus Christ in China today as an institution, or collection of institutions, is nonexistent, a helpless victim of the powerful and remorseless materialistic and political forces of the twentieth century. These forces are unlikely to be materially diminished, let alone spent, within the next two decades in any Asian country. But the Church of Jesus Christ in China today as a living, vital organism continues to exist and even grow triumphantly, despite the persecutions, the limitations, the frustrations imposed by a despotic totalitarian government.

If, short of Bibles, bereft of institutions, deprived of fellowship, cut off from all outside help and consolation for twenty years, the Church of Jesus Christ in China can live and grow and be a threat to the beliefs and practices of the most materialistic totalitarianism the world has ever known, how immense are the possibilities of this Church, not only in China but in all countries, in all its members, in all its gifts and graces and power, if allowed to express itself as God intended in the second half of the twentieth century!

NOTES

Preface
1. C. K. Yang, *Religion in Chinese Society* (Berkeley: University of California Press, 1961), p. 387.
2. *Time,* January 8, 1951.
3. C. K. Yang, *op. cit.,* p. 386.
4. Edward Rogers, *A Christian Commentary on Communism* (London: Epworth Press, 1959), p. 208.
5. See Bonnie Compton, *A Young Man's Choice* (Wheaton, Ill.: Scripture Press Publications, 1962).
6. I have recounted these events in *God's Fool* (London: Faber and Faber, 1954; New York: Doubleday and Co., 1954).
7. He tells his story in *When Iron Gates Yield* (Chicago: Moody Press, 1954).

Chapter One
1. II Corinthians 9:6; II Thessalonians 3:10.

Chapter Two
1. Kenneth Scott Latourette, *A History of Christian Missions in China* (London: S.P.C.K., 1929; New York: Russell & Russell [1929], 1967), pp. 48-49. A. C. Moule, *Christians in China Before the Year 1550* (London: S.P.C.K., 1930), pp. 1-24.
2. Latourette, *op. cit.,* p. 49.
3. Moule, *op. cit.,* p. 27.
4. Latourette, *op. cit.,* p. 52. A full translation of the Nestorian Monument from *The History of the Great and Renowned Monarchy of China* by Fr. Alvarez Semedo (London, 1655), is given in Columba Cary-Elwes, *China and the Cross* (London: Longmans, Green & Co., 1957; New York: P. J. Kenedy & Sons, 1957), Appendix I. Moule, *op. cit.,* also has a complete translation, pp. 34-52.
5. Marshall Broomhall, *The Chinese Empire: A General and Missionary Survey* (London: Marshall, Morgan and Scott, 1907), p. 6.
6. Latourette, *op. cit.,* p. 54.
7. *Ibid.,* p. 37.
8. T. J. Ryan, S. J., *Jesuits in China* (Hong Kong: Catholic Truth Society), p. 12.
9. Fr. Matteo Ricci, *Commentari,* quoted in Cary-Elwes, *op. cit.,* pp. 88-90.
10. Ryan, *op. cit.,* p. 52.
11. *Ibid.,* p. 67.
12. Cary-Elwes, *op. cit.,* p. 212; Latourette, *op. cit.,* p. 479.

13. See George Patterson, *The Unquiet Frontier* (London: Dragonfly Paperback, 1967).

14. Cary-Elwes, *op. cit.*, pp. 212-215.

15. Latourette, *op. cit.*, p. 261.

16. Timothy Richard, *Forty-Five Years in China* (New York: Frederick A. Stokes Company, 1916), p. 133.

17. *Ibid.*, p. 143.

18. Broomhall, *op. cit.*, p. 18.

19. Kenneth Scott Latourette, *Christianity in a Revolutionary Age,* Vol. III (London: Eyre & Spottiswoode, 1961; New York: Harper & Row, Inc., 1961), p. 439.

20. *Ibid.*, pp. 439ff.

21. *Ibid.*, pp. 441, 442. See also Latourette, *History of Missions in China,* p. 680.

22. This and other quotations of treaties are from *Histoire Generale de la Chine,* Vol. IV, pp. 111-114, quoted in Cary-Elwes, *op. cit.*, pp. 198-199.

23. Tables taken from Broomhall, *op. cit.*, pp. 35, 40.

24. *Ibid.*, p. 19.

25. Latourette, *Christianity in a Revolutionary Age,* p. 435.

26. *China Year Book, 1963-64* (Taiwan: China Publishing Company, 1964), pp. 99-104. *Les Missions de Chine* (Shanghai: The Lazarist Fathers, 1941).

27. *China Year Book, 1963-64,* pp. 99-104. Also *China Year Book, 1939.*

28. Cary-Elwes, *op. cit.*, p. 256.

29. *Ibid.*, pp. 255-256.

30. Francis P. Jones, *The Church in Communist China: A Protestant Appraisal* (New York: Friendship Press, 1962), pp. 16-20.

31. Latourette, *Christianity in a Revolutionary Age,* p. 445.

Chapter Three

1. Cary-Elwes, *op. cit.*, p. 266.

2. C. P. Fitzgerald, *The Birth of Communist China* (Harmondsworth, Middlesex: Penguin Books, Ltd.; Baltimore, Md.: Penguin Books, 1964), p. 135. This was originally published by The Cresset Press, London.

3. A. J. Dain, Editor, *Mission Fields Today* (London: Inter-Varsity Fellowship, 1956), pp. 21, 22.

4. Paul A. Varg, *Missionaries, Chinese Diplomats: The American Protestant Missionary Movement in China* (Princeton, N.J.: Princeton University Press, 1958), pp. 294-302.

5. Fitzgerald, *op. cit.*, p. 136.

6. David N. Paton, *Christian Missions and the Judgment of God* (London: S. C. M. Press, 1953), p. 37.

7. Leslie T. Lyall, *Come Wind, Come Weather* (Chicago: Moody Press, 1960), p. 13. London: Hodder & Stoughton. Used by permission. Moody Press, Moody Bible Institute of Chicago; Hodder and Stoughton.

8. Dain, *op. cit.*, p. 23.

9. Helen Willis, *Through Encouragement of the Scriptures* (Hong Kong: Christian Book Room, 1963), pp. 16-17.

10. Jones, *op. cit.*, p. 52.

11. "Message from Chinese Christians to Mission Boards Abroad," quoted in full in Francis P. Jones, Editor, *Documents of the Three-Self Movement* (New York: National Council of Churches, East Asia Department, 1963), pp. 14-18.

12. *Ibid.,* p. 20.

13. For a critical discussion of the rights and wrongs of "imperialism" see Maurice Zinkin, *Asia and the West* (London: Chatto and Windus, 1951).

14. Paton, *op. cit.,* pp. 36-38.

15. Lyall, *op. cit.,* pp. 16-17.

16. *Ibid.,* pp. 23, 34; Jones, *The Church in Communist China,* pp. 57, 58.

17. Cary-Elwes, *op. cit.,* p. 267.

18. *Ibid.,* p. 270.

19. *Ibid.,* pp. 272-274, with quotations from *The Tablet.*

20. *A People's Democratic Dictatorship,* published in July, 1949.

21. Harold H. Martinson, *Red Dragon Over China* (Minneapolis: Augsburg Publishing House, 1956), p. 153. Quoted by permission of Augsburg Publishing House, Minneapolis, copyright owner.

22. Willis, *op. cit.,* pp. 125-126.

Chapter Four

1. Varg, *op. cit.,* p. 3.

2. *China Mission Year Book, 1923* (Shanghai: Christian Literature Society, 1923).

3. Latourette, *History of Missions in China,* pp. 795, 796; Varg, *op. cit.,* pp. 212, 213.

4. Varg, *op. cit.,* pp. 213-214. See *Laymen's Enquiry* papers memorandum on "China Sunday School Union," 1929, Missionary Research Library, New York.

5. "Can Christian Missions Be Saved?" *Christian Century,* March 12, 1930. Varg, *op. cit.,* p. 214.

6. Varg, *op. cit.,* p. 214.

7. *Bulletin of the China Committee,* April 11, 1947, quoted in Varg, *op. cit.,* p. 279.

8. Varg, *op. cit.,* pp. 282, 283.

9. F. Olin Stockwell, *With God in Red China: The Story of Two Years in Communist Prisons* (New York: Harper & Row, Inc., 1953), pp. 30, 28-29, and elsewhere.

10. Varg, *op cit.,* pp. 292, 293.

11. *Ibid.,* p. 309.

12. Jones, ed., *Documents,* pp. 1-5.

13. "How My Political Thinking Has Changed," Jones, ed., *Documents,* pp. 55-59.

14. Quoted from Edward G. Nelson, "Christianity in China," *The Covenant Weekly* (now *Covenant Companion*), April 8, 1955.

15. Varg, *op. cit.,* pp. 311-312.

16. Stockwell, *op. cit.,* p. 61.

17. Glenn D. Kittler, *The Maryknoll Fathers* (New York: All Saints Press, Inc., 1963), pp. 297-298.

18. *Ibid.*

19. Lyall, *op. cit.*, p. 20.
20. Jones, *The Church in Communist China*, p. 59; Stockwell, *op. cit.*, pp. 186-187, 191-194.
21. "The First Eight Months of the Three-Self Movement," quoted in Jones, ed., *Documents*, pp. 34-40. The Three-Self Reform Movement was considered to have begun with the issuing of the Manifesto.
22. Jones, *The Church in Communist China*, pp. 64, 65.
23. Lyall, *op. cit.*, p. 30.
24. Edward Hunter, *The Story of Mary Liu* (New York: Farrar, Straus, and Cudahy, 1957), pp. 185-211.
25. Lyall, *op. cit.*, pp. 31, 32.
26. *Ibid.*, pp. 32, 36.
27. "United Declaration of the Delegates of Chinese Christian Churches and Church Institutions," quoted in Jones, ed., *op. cit.*, pp. 41-43.
28. Varg., *op. cit.*, p. 315.
29. Jean Monsterleet, *Martyrs in China*, translated by Antonia Pakenham, (Chicago: Henry Regnery, 1956), pp. 251-252.
30. William Sargant, *Battle for the Mind* (New York: Doubleday & Co., Inc., 1957).
31. The comparison is noted by Varg, *op. cit.*, p. 313, and more generally by Fitzgerald, *op. cit.*, pp. 140, 145-152.
32. Geoffrey T. Bull, *When Iron Gates Yield* (London: Hodder & Stoughton; Chicago: Moody Press; 1955), p. 177. Used by permission. Moody Press, Moody Bible Institute of Chicago; Hodder & Stoughton.
33. *Ibid.*, pp. 180-187, *passim*.
34. *Ibid.*, p. 204.
35. Quoted in Lyall, *op. cit.*, p. 41.
36. *Tien Feng*, January 15, 1953, quoted in Lyall, *op. cit.*, p. 22.
37. *Tien Feng*, July 7, 1951, quoted in Jones, ed., *Documents*, pp. 51-54.

Chapter Five
1. Jones, *The Church in Communist China*, p. 17. The account of Isaac Wei's confession that follows is taken from Jones, ed., *Documents*, pp. 60-65.
2. *Ibid.*
3. Lyall, *op. cit.*, p. 64.
4. This account of the Jesus Family, and the quotations, are taken from D. Vaughan Rees, *The "Jesus Family" In Communist China* (London: Paternoster Press, 1959), pp. 14-64, *passim*.
5. Jones, *The Church in Communist China*, p. 18.
6. Paton, *op. cit.*, pp. 28-29.
7. *Ibid.*, pp. 48-49.
8. Rees, *op. cit.*, p. 18.
9. *Ibid.*, p. 26.
10. Lyall, *op. cit.*, pp. 41, 42.

Chapter Six
1. *South China Morning Post*, January 11, 1953.

2. Liu Shao-chi, *On the Party* (Peking: Foreign Languages Press, 1950), pp. 57-58.

3. *China Notes,* September, 1962 (New York: The Chinese Committee, National Council of Churches).

4. *Ibid.,* p. 2.

5. Peking, New China News Agency (NCNA), August 6, 1954. Quoted in full in Jones, ed., *Documents,* pp. 85-95.

6. Peking, *China News Service,* August 13, 1954.

7. *Ibid.*

8. *Tien Feng,* September 3, 1954; Jones, ed., *Documents,* p. 92.

9. Quoted in Jones, ed., *Documents,* pp. 98-99.

10. Peking, NCNA, August 14, 1954.

11. *China Notes, op. cit.,* p. 3.

12. *Ibid.,* p. 4.

13. *Ibid.*

14. Quoted in Jones, ed., *Documents,* pp. 156-167.

15. *China Notes, op. cit.,* p. 5.

16. *Tien Feng,* March 31, 1958.

17. Jones, *The Church in Communist China,* pp. 150-151.

18. *China Notes, op. cit.,* p. 5.

19. *Ibid.*

20. *Tien Feng,* January-February, 1961, quoted in Jones, ed., *Documents,* pp. 198-199.

21. *Tien Feng,* January-February, 1961. A condensed version is given in Jones, ed., *Documents,* pp. 194-198.

22. *Tien Feng,* No. 17-18, 1962, p. 25.

Chapter Seven

1. "A True Realization of the Question of the Catholic and Protestant Churches," *Current Affairs Journal,* No. 3, 1950. Reproduced by Peking, NCNA, November 23, 1950.

2. *Ibid.*

3. *The Catholic Church in China* (Research Background), P.O. Box 5217, Kowloon, Hong Kong.

4. Peking, NCNA, December 12, 1950.

5. *Ibid.*

6. *The Catholic Church in China,* pp. 78-79.

7. Paul K. T. Sik, *Decision for China: Communism or Christianity* (Chicago: Henry Regnery Company, 1959), p. 144.

8. *China Missionary Bulletin,* Hong Kong, Vol. V (January 1953), p. 1.

9. *Ibid.,* pp. 2-4.

10. Lyall, *op. cit.,* p. 35.

11. *The Catholic Church in China,* p. 106.

12. *Ibid.,* p. 107.

13. Changsha, *Hsiu Hunan Pao,* June 3, 1957; *People's China,* July 1, 1957, pp. 3-27.

14. Peking, *People's Daily,* December 24, 1957.

15. *The Catholic Church in China,* p. 88.

16. Wuhan, *Chang Chiang Jih Pao,* April 18, 1958.

17. *Ibid.*

18. *The Catholic Church in China,* p. i.
19. Peking, *People's Daily,* April 15, 1960.
20. Peking, *Nationalities Unity Monthly* (*Min Tsu Tuan Chi*), April, 1962, pp. 2-5.

Chapter Eight
1. Berkeley: University of California Press, 1961, p. 339.
2. "Atheists and Theists Can Co-operate Politically and Travel the Road to Socialism," *Current Background* (Hong Kong: United States Information Service), No. 510, June 15, 1968.
3. *Ibid.*
4. *America,* August 11, 1956.
5. Glenn D. Kittler, *The Maryknoll Fathers* (New York: All Saints Press, Inc., 1963), p. 291.
6. *China Missionary Bulletin,* Vol. V, January 1953, p. 2.
7. *Ibid.,* Vol. IV, October 1952, p. 648.
8. *America,* August 11, 1956, p. 442.
9. Lyall, *op. cit.,* pp. 52-58.
10. *Ibid.,* pp. 38-51, *passim;* Jones, *Church in Communist China,* pp. 103ff.
11. Lyall, *op. cit.,* p. 38.
12. *Ibid.,* pp. 45-46.
13. Jones, ed., *Documents,* p. 117.
14. Jones, *Church in Communist China,* p. 105.
15. *Ibid.,* pp. 106-109.
16. Lyall, *op. cit.,* pp. 64-66.
17. A *Tien Feng* editorial quoted in Jones, *Church in Communist China,* p. 109.
18. Lyall, *op. cit.,* p. 66.
19. Jones, *Church in Communist China,* pp. 108-109.
20. *Ibid.*
21. Lyall, *op. cit.,* pp. 66-67.
22. Jones, ed., *Documents,* pp. 121-133.
23. *Ibid.,* pp. 133-135.
24. Jones, *The Church in Communist China,* pp. 131-132.
25. *Catholic Sunday Examiner,* Hong Kong, November 30, 1958, p. 8.
26. Thomas J. Bauer, M. M., *The Systematic Destruction of the Catholic Church in China* (New York: World Horizon Reports, 1954).
27. Union Research Service, Hong Kong, October 11, 1955, p. 1.
28. Kenneth Scott Latourette, *Christianity in a Revolutionary Age,* Vol. V (New York: Harper & Row, Inc., 1962), p. 398.
29. Kittler, *op. cit.,* p. 3.
30. Jones, ed., *Documents,* pp. 151-156.
31. Lyall, *op. cit.,* p. 70.
32. *Ibid.,* pp. 76-77; Jones, *The Church in Communist China,* pp. 146-147.
33. Jones, *The Church in Communist China,* pp. 153-154.
34. Jones, ed., *Documents,* pp. 183-184.
35. Quoted in Lyall, *op. cit.,* p. 86.
36. Y. T. Wu, "A Glorious Ten Years," Jones, ed., *Documents,* pp. 192-194.

Chapter Nine
1. Jones, ed., *Documents,* p. 198.
2. *Kwangming Daily,* June 30, 1965.
3. Peking, *People's Daily,* April 8, 1963.
4. *Kwangming Daily,* April 2, 1964.
5. *China Notes,* 109, April 1, 1965.
6. *Ibid.*
7. *China Youth,* No. 2, January 16, 1965.
8. *Canton Southern Daily,* December 18, 1964.
9. Peking, *People's Daily,* April 20, 1965.
10. *China Youth,* July 1, 1965.
11. *Ibid.*
12. *Ibid.*
13. *South China Morning Post,* August 16, 1966.
14. *Kwangming Daily,* March 7, 1965.
15. *China Reconstructs,* January 1958, Jones, ed., *Documents,* pp. 175-176.

Chapter Ten
1. "There is a great deal of talk in Church circles at the present time about the importance of the laity. But the question is almost invariably approached from the wrong end. What is usually meant is that more laymen should come in and give their support to the Church as it is. That is just what a large number of the best lay people at present standing on the fringe will not do." J. A. Oldham, *Life Is Commitment* (New York: Association Press, 1959), p. 89.

Every effort has been made to identify sources of information and quotations. If there have been any omissions or oversights, the author and publisher will be glad to give credit in subsequent editions.

APPENDIX I

The Christian Manifesto *

Direction of Endeavor for Chinese Christianity in the Construction of New China, May, 1950

Protestant Christianity has been introduced to China for more than a hundred and forty years. During this period it has made a not unworthy contribution to Chinese society. Nevertheless, and this was most unfortunate, not long after Christianity's coming to China, imperialism started its activities here; and since the principal groups of missionaries who brought Christianity to China all came themselves from these imperialistic countries. Christianity consciously or unconsciously, directly or indirectly, became related with imperialism. Now that the Chinese revolution has achieved victory, these imperialistic countries will not rest passively content in face of this unprecedented historical fact in China. They will certainly seek to contrive by every means the destruction of what has actually been achieved; they may also make use of Christianity to forward their plot of stirring up internal dissension, and creating reactionary forces in this country. It is our purpose in publishing the following statement to heighten our vigilance against imperialism, to make the clear political stand of Christians in New China, to hasten the building of a Chinese church whose affairs are managed by the Chinese themselves, and to indicate the responsibilities that should be taken up by Christians throughout the whole country in national reconstruction in New China. We desire to call upon all Christians in the country to exert their best efforts in putting into effect the principles herein presented.

The Task in General

Christian Churches and organizations give thoroughgoing support to the "Common Political Platform," and under the leadership of the government oppose imperialism, feudalism, and bureaucratic capitalism, and take part in the effort to build an independent, democratic, peaceable, unified, prosperous, and powerful New China.

---

*Quoted from Jones, ed., *Documents of the Three-Self Movement*, pp. 19-20.

Fundamental Aims

(1) Christian churches and organizations in China should exert their utmost efforts, and employ effective methods, to make people in the churches everywhere recognize clearly the evils that have been wrought in China by imperialism; recognize the fact that in the past imperialism has made use of Christianity itself; and be vigilant against imperialism, and especially American imperialism, in its plot to use religion in fostering the growth of reactionary forces. At the same time, the churches and organizations should call upon Christians to participate in the movement opposing war and upholding peace, and teach them thoroughly to understand and support the government's policy of agrarian reform.

(2) Christian churches and organizations in China should take effective measures to cultivate a patriotic and democratic spirit among their adherents in general, as well as a psychology of self-respect and self-reliance. The movement of autonomy, self-support, and self-propagation hitherto promoted in the Chinese church has already attained a measure of success. This movement from now onward should complete its tasks within the shortest possible period. At the same time, self-criticism should be advocated, all forms of Christian activity reexamined and readjusted, and thoroughgoing austerity measures adopted, so as to achieve the goals of a reformation in the church.

Concrete Methods

(1) All Christian churches and organizations in China that are still relying upon foreign personnel and financial aid should work out concrete plans to realize within the shortest possible time their objective of self-reliance and rejuvenation.

(2) From now onward, as regards their religious work, Christian churches and organizations should lay emphasis upon a deeper understanding of the nature of Christianity itself, closer fellowship and unity among the various denominations, the cultivation of better leadership personnel, and reform in systems of church organization. As regards their more general work, they should emphasize anti-imperialistic, anti-feudalistic and anti-bureaucratic-capitalistic education, together with such forms of service to the people as productive labor, teaching them to understand the New Era, cultural and recreational activities, literacy education, medical and public health work, and care of children.

Peking Edict of December 29, 1950*

Regulations Governing All Organizations Subsidized With Foreign Funds

Promulgated by the 65th Session of the State Administrative Council, Chou En-lai, Chairman, Peking, December 29, 1950. Text as given by New China News Agency.

1. In order to control effectively the funds from foreign sources sent into China for the support of Cultural, Educational, Relief, and Religious work, the following regulations are promulgated.

2. The regulations are for those who receive foreign funds for the support of Cultural, Educational, Relief, and Religious work, and especially for the Chinese groups which receive these funds whether they be as gifts or as fixed budgets, and regardless of whether they are given by private sources or social groups, or whether it be for partial support or for full support. The groups are as follows:

a) Universities, Colleges, High Schools, Primary Schools, Kindergartens, Blind and Deaf and Dumb Schools and others.

b) Hospitals, Sanatoriums, Leprosariums, Ambulance Corps, and other medical units.

c) Religious Bodies and their affiliated organizations.

d) Orphanages, Old People's Homes, Children's Homes, and other social services.

e) Printing Houses, Publishing Societies, and Book Stores.

f) Libraries and Broadcasting stations.

g) Cultural Groups and Study Organizations.

3. In regard to the above-mentioned organizations and their work, they must follow the regulations promulgated by the Government, each according to the various type of work. Each must register under their respective bureau, as for example Schools under the Educational Bureau, and medical, social service, and industrial work under their respective

---

*Taken from Jones, ed., *Documents of the Three-Self Movement*, pp. 22-24.

bureaus. Besides this they must be registered with a Special Committee of the Local, City, and Provincial People's Government. In making this registration the important thing in each type of work is: The Organization's Name, Locations, Name of the responsible Leader, his Age, his Nationality, his History, his Capital, as well as his subsidies with their amount and their source, nature of work and conditions for use of funds, as well as a detailed concrete plan.

4. In order to facilitate the registration of the groups mentioned above, a Special Registration Office shall be set up under the Municipal or Provincial People's Government to give special attention to all receiving and handling funds and foreign grants for Cultural, Educational, Relief and Religious work.

5. Each group specified under Paragraph Two must be obedient to the rules of the Common Programme, and to all the laws of the Government, and must not do anything that is in opposition to the interests of the people. They must observe the following:

a. Every six months they must submit in writing to the Special Committee of the respective Municipal and Provincial People's Government a report of the subsidies and funds received for the support of Cultural, Educational, Relief, and Religious work, as well as a statement of the manner in which the funds are used.

b. If funds intended for one place or one type of work are remitted or used for work in some other place, or whenever funds arrive from a foreign land, such matters must be reported in advance to the Local, Municipal, and Provincial Committee which is authorized to handle gifts and grants for Cultural, Educational, Relief, and Religious work.

6. Whoever violates the above regulations or secretly does not notify the proper authorities, or makes a false report, and is later discovered by the authorities, shall be punished. If the offence is regarded as grave, the taking over, reorganization, or forced closure shall be effected upon the ratification of the upper-level People's Government.

7. If after three months following the promulgation of these regulations it is found that the above-mentioned organizations or groups have not registered, they shall be subject to investigation by the local authorities and liable to penalty by the local People's Government.

8. All Cultural, Educational, Relief, and Religious Organizations registered according to the stipulations of the present regulations, who have truly severed all connections with foreign countries and shall have reported that the Special Committee of the Local, Municipal or Provincial Committee, shall be released from the regulations governing the Special registration.

9. Measures for the enforcement of the present regulations shall be formulated separately by the Committee on Cultural and Educational Affairs of the State Administrative Council.

10. The Regulations shall be enforced upon promulgation by the Premier's Administrative Council of the Central People's Government.

How to Hold a Successful Accusation Meeting *

Written by Liu Liang-mo. Text as given by the New China News Agency of Shanghai for May 15, 1951.

One of the central tasks at present for Christian churches and groups across the nation is to hold successful accusation meetings.

Why do we want to accuse? Because for more than a hundred years imperialism has utilized Christianity to attack China, therefore we want to accuse it of its sins. As a result of the longtime influence of imperialism, many Christians have the old-fashioned idea of "being above politics"; therefore we must hold accusation meetings to educate everybody. Big accusation meetings constitute a most effective means of helping the masses of believers to comprehend the evils wrought in China by imperialism, to recognize the fact that imperialism has utilized Christianity to attack China, and to wipe out imperialist influences within the churches.

Accuse what? We must accuse imperialist elements and their helpers as well as other bad elements hidden in the churches. We want to expose their sin of utilizing the churches to attack China and deceive believers. For example, many Christians in Tsingtao, Shanghai, Hangchow and Peking have accused America's political agent, Ku Jen-en, of wearing the cloak of religion to engage in counter-revolutionary activities, and even rumor-mongering and swindling, raping women and killing sick people. Christian leaders such as Ts'ui Hsien-hsiang and Chiang Ch'ang-ch'uan have accused imperialist elements, Frank Price, etc., who take the name of missionary to carry on special agent activities, and other special agents of America and Chiang who hold high positions in the churches.

How shall we hold a successful accusation meeting? First, we must remove the thought barriers of many Christians. Some Christians suppose that they ought to "hide evil and display good" or that they ought not to accuse. And yet Jesus' reprimands to the scribes and Pharisees of that time were certainly accusations. Some Christians feel that they are "unable to accuse of some things"; they ought then to participate more in

---

*Taken from Jones, ed., *Documents of the Three-Self Movement*, pp. 49-51.

the big accusation meetings of people from all walks of life and the public trials of counter-revolutionaries. The anger and charges of the masses of the people towards imperialism, bandits, and wicked tyrants will arouse the righteous indignation and accusations of Christians towards imperialism and bad elements in the churches.

Second, if we want to hold a successful accusation meeting, we must first do well the preparatory work. Every church and the city-wide church federation ought to first organize an accusation committee. They should first study whom they want to accuse, and whom to invite to do the accusing. After this they should invite those participating in the accusation to attend a meeting to mobilize accusations so that they may understand why, what and how they should accuse. The second step of the preparation work is to hold in every church and group preliminary accusation meetings. In these meetings we should urge everyone to enthusiastically express his opinions and accuse. In this way we shall be able to discover a few people who accuse with the greatest power and invite them to participate in the large accusation meeting and can also correct certain weaknesses in their speaking, for example,. making briefer the speeches which are too long, making clearer the speeches which are unclear, and making fuller the content of those which are insufficient.

Third, what can be considered to be a successful accusation meeting? According to the experience of Ts'ui Hsien-Hsiang, who accused Frank Price, accusations (1) ought to be according to facts, (2) must break through all sentimentality; (3) must in every sentence be spoken from the depths of the heart; (4) must be thorough-going, outspoken, sincere and uninhibited; (5) must hold firmly to the position of the people. Bishop Chiang Ch'ang-ch'uan of the Methodist Church, when he accused that bad element of the church, Ch'en Wen-Yuan, said: "I am determined to purge my church in the spirit of unmitigated punishment of offenders, no matter who they are, definitely cleaning out thoroughly all elements like Ch'en Wen-yuan; if there is one, remove one, if there are ten, remove ten!" This sort of accusation moves people very deeply.

Fourth, the atmosphere of the meeting must be dignified when carrying on a local church or city-wide accusation meeting. The order of arrangement of the accusers is very important; they should be arranged as follows: first high tension,. then moderate, then another of high tension, etc.; only so can the accusation meeting be a success. When the accusations have succeeded in deeply stirring people, clapping and applause may be used as a form of expression. Throughout the whole process of preparation for the big accusation meeting, we ought to invite the Religious Affairs Bureau of the local People's Government or other related offices, democratic political groups and other concerned parties to come and advise. The texts of outstanding accusations ought to be recorded and given to local papers for publishing, and also mailed to the Preparation Committee of the Chinese Christian Oppose-America Assist-Korea Three-Self Reform Movement Committee (address: 131 Museum Road, Shanghai). If there is evidence of specific crimes of imperialist elements or bad elements in the churches, such as correspondence, pictures, weapons, radios, etc., these must be reported to the local police office; and after obtaining the agreement of the police office, we may open a local exhibit of concrete materials, or mail them directly to the Preparation Committee of the Chinese Christian Oppose-America Assist-Korea Three-Self Reform Movement Committee for use in a nationwide exhibition.

What about after the accusation? After the accusation the patriotic fervor and political comprehension of the masses of believers will be raised and they will have a much clearer understanding of imperialism. We ought to encourage the whole body of workers and fellow-believers in the church and all Christians to carry out the following tasks: (1) Strengthen study of current affairs; (2) Continue promoting the Three-Self Reform Movement; (3) Continue cleaning out all imperialist and bad elements within the churches; (4) Participate in local and national movements for the suppression of counter-revolution; (5) and actively participate in the Oppose-America Assist-Korea movement.

To hold a successful big accusation meeting is one of the important tasks that every church must do well to wipe out the influence of imperialism!

APPENDIX IV

Father, long before creation
Thou hadst chosen us in love;
And that love, so deep, so moving,
Draws us close to Christ above.
    Still it keeps us,
    Still it keeps us,
Firmly fixed in Christ alone.

Though the world may change its fashion
Yet our God is e'er the same,
His compassion and His covenant
Through all ages will remain
    God's own children,
    God's own children,
Must forever praise His name.

God's compassion is my story,
Is my boasting all the day;
Mercy free and never failing
Moves my will, directs my way.
    Go so loved us,
    Go so loved us,
That His only Son He gave.

Loving Father, now before Thee
We will ever praise Thy love;
And our song will sound unceasing
Till we reach our home above,
    Giving glory
    Giving glory
To our God and to the Lord.

Translation by Francis Price Jones. May be sung to Welsh tune of *Cwm Rhondda,* or to *Miller Chapel* by David Hugh Jones (in *The Hymnbook*).

Given in Jones, ed., *Documents of the Three-Self Movement*, p. 73.

174